RECORDER

GRADES 5–6

SPOTLIGHT on MUSIC™

SERIES AUTHORS

Judy Bond
René Boyer
Margaret Campbelle-Holman
Emily Crocker
Marilyn C. Davidson
Robert de Frece
Virginia Ebinger
Mary Goetze
Betsy M. Henderson
John Jacobson
Michael Jothen
Chris Judah-Lauder
Carol King
Vincent P. Lawrence
Ellen McCullough-Brabson
Janet McMillion
Nancy L.T. Miller
Ivy Rawlins
Susan Snyder
Gilberto D. Soto

Kodály Contributing Consultant
Sr. Lorna Zemke

Mc Graw Hill Macmillan McGraw-Hill

NOTE TO THE TEACHER

Spotlight on Music: Recorder contains soprano and alto recorder activities for Macmillan/McGraw-Hill's SPOTLIGHT™ ON MUSIC, Grades 5 and 6. The activities are blackline masters that can be duplicated for student use. You may wish to create overhead transparencies to use in addition to, or in place of, individual copies. Teaching suggestions are on the back of each blackline master. Lessons 1–18 are correlated to SPOTLIGHT™ ON MUSIC, Grade 5. Lessons 19–36 are correlated to Grade 6.

This resource contains the following:

- Fingering charts.
- Practice patterns, teaching suggestions, and tips on recorder technique.
- Playalongs, harmony parts, and ensemble work.
- Opportunities for student improvisation.
- Creative activities related to songs in the blackline masters.

Recorder playing reinforces a wide range of musical skills, including note-reading and music theory. In addition, it provides an excellent foundation for participation in your school's instrumental music program.

ACKNOWLEDGMENTS

Grateful acknowledgement is given to the following authors, composers, and publishers. Every effort has been made to trace the ownership of all copyrighted material and to secure the necessary permissions to reprint these selections.

Guantanamera, Original lyrics and music by José Fernandez Diaz (Joseito Fernandez), Music adaptation by Pete Seeger, Lyric adaptation by Hector Angulo, based on a poem by José Martí. © Copyright 1963, 1965 by Fall River Music, Inc. New York, NY. Copyright Renewed. International Copyright Secured. All Rights Reserved.

Rock Around the Clock, Words and Music by Max C. Freedman and Jimmy DeKnight. Copyright © 1953. Myers Music Inc. and Capano Music. Copyright Renewed 1981. All Rights on behalf of Myers Music Inc. Administered by Sony/ATV Music Publishing, 8 Music Square West, Nashville, TN 37203. International Copyright Secured. All Rights Reserved.

Yellow Bird, Words and Music by Irving Burgie. Copyright © 1957; Renewed 1985 Cherry Lane Music Publishing Company, Inc. (ASCAP), Lord Burgess Music Publishing (ASCAP) and DreamWorks Songs (ASCAP) Worldwide Rights for Lord Burgess Music Publishing and DreamWorks Songs, Administered by Cherry Lane Music Publishing Company, Inc. International Copyright Secured. All Rights Reserved.

Writer
Virginia Ebinger

B

The McGraw·Hill Companies

Published by Macmillan/McGraw-Hill, of McGraw-Hill Education, a division of The McGraw-Hill Companies, Inc., Two Penn Plaza, New York, New York 10121.

Printed in the United States of America

7 8 9 10 11 12 024 10 09 08

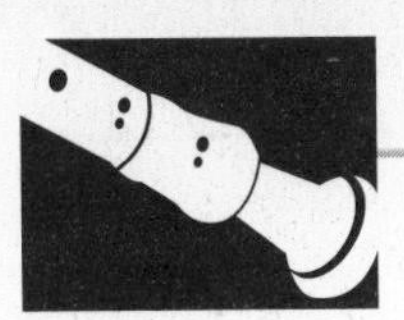

Table of Contents

Table of Contents (Continued)

Name ______________________ Date ______________

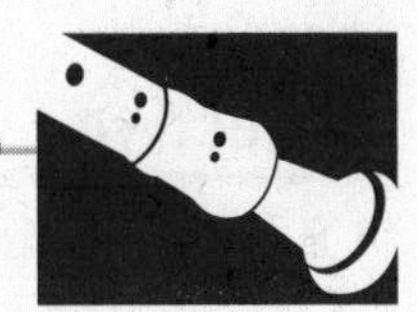

In the Bag

Most people begin playing the recorder by learning these notes.

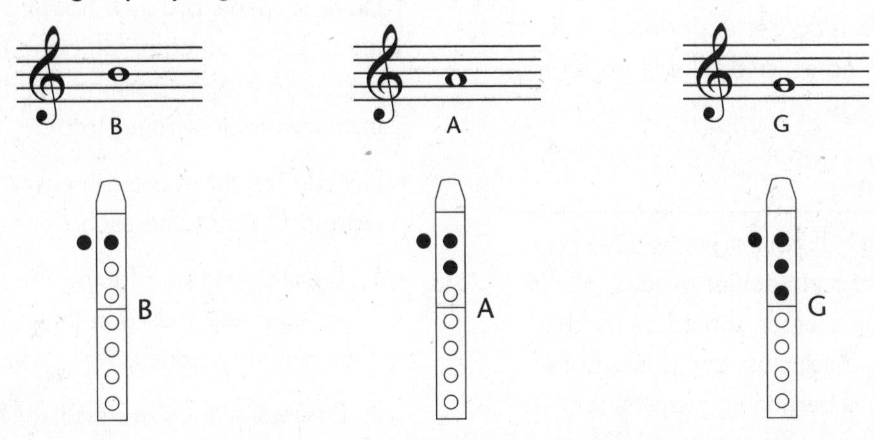

- Watch and listen as your teacher shows you proper posture and the correct way to hold the recorder. The three most important things to think about as you begin to play the recorder are:
  Your breath
  Your fingers
  Your ears
- Pick up your recorder with your left hand. Hold it as you held your "arm recorder." Cover the hole on the back with your left thumb and the top hole on the front with your pointer finger. This is the fingering for B. Support the recorder lightly with your right hand at the bottom. Now sit tall and hold your recorder straight down in front of you.
- Place the mouthpiece on your lower lip, then close your upper lip around it. Don't let it touch your teeth. Breathe gently into the recorder a whispered *doo*. Echo patterns your teacher plays on B.
- Using the fingering charts above, follow your teacher to learn A and G. Practice playing echoes on B, A and G with a partner.
- Now the whole class can play "Hot Cross Buns."

Pitches: B A G

Using Recorder Master R • 1

Objective

- Beginning students will learn correct posture, holding position, and fingering for B, A, and G.
- Students with recorder experience will review these notes, and all will perform in two playalongs.

Preparation

(Note to Teacher: If your students have had recorder instruction in earlier grades, all the information in this lesson should be used only if needed. If the class comprises both experienced and beginning players, use material as a review for some and beginning instruction for the others. Refer to earlier lessons in *Spotlight on Music, Recorder,* Grades 3–4.)

- Discuss the basic principles of learning to play any instrument: start slowly and carefully, and learn basic techniques correctly to avoid future problems.
- Introduce the "arm recorder": Put right arm in the air and make right hand into fist. Place right fist under chin, elbow down. Right wrist now serves as "arm recorder," helpful in teaching proper holding technique.
- Explain how to finger B.
- Have students place thumb on pulse at the back of wrist, then place index finger opposite thumb on front of wrist.
- Have students feel finger pads, the flat, fleshy part of the fingers. This part of the fingers covers the holes of the recorder. These holes must be completely covered.

Procedure

- Have students pick up recorder with left hand and hold in position of "arm recorder," left thumb on back hole, index, pointer, and ring fingers over top three holes; right hand at the bottom of the recorder, thumb supporting from the back of the recorder.
- Have students practice holding the recorder mouthpiece on chin, left hand thumb and fingers in proper position, when listening to instructions or waiting to play.
- Explain the three most important things in learning to play the recorder.
  1. Breath—When placing the recorder's mouthpiece between their lips, breathe into it very gently, whispering *doo*.
  2. Fingers—Place the pads of fingers straight across the proper holes, covering them completely.
  3. Ears—Always listen very carefully to the sounds they make on their recorders.
- Review the basics of recorder technique.
  1. Place the mouthpiece between the lips.
  2. Keep the left hand at the top.
  3. Breathe very gently into the recorder.
  4. Tongue with a whispered *doo*.
- Play short patterns on B for students to echo. Then have students play B on each downbeat while you play "Hot Cross Buns."
- Demonstrate fingering for A, then play short phrases on B and A for students to echo.
- Guide students through B and A piece, fingering it on their recorders while singing the pitch names, finally playing it.
- Demonstrate fingering for G, then play short phrases on B, A and G for students to echo.
- Guide students in playing "Hot Cross Buns."

Name ______________________ Date ______________

Two Hands Are Better Than One

So far you have used your right hand only to support your recorder, an important function, especially when you are playing the notes B A G, but it has many other responsibilities also.

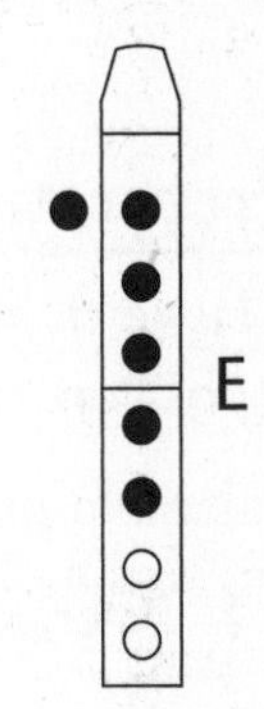

- Echo the B A G patterns your teacher or a classmate plays.
- Place your right thumb about one-third of the way up from the bottom, on the back of the recorder, with your right fingers just above the holes on the front. With your left hand in position for G cover the next *two* holes with your right pointer and middle fingers. Now when you breathe into your recorder the sound you hear will be E.
- Practice going back and forth between G and E. Be sure to place the appropriate fingers on the holes at the same time—all at once.
- Learn procedure for three-part echo: listen, sing pitch names while fingering silently, play.
- Perform three-part echoes on your teacher's B A G E patterns.
- Practice echoes with a partner.
- First sing the pitch names and finger the notes silently, then play the two pieces below:

- Make your own four-measure piece using B A G E. Write it below.

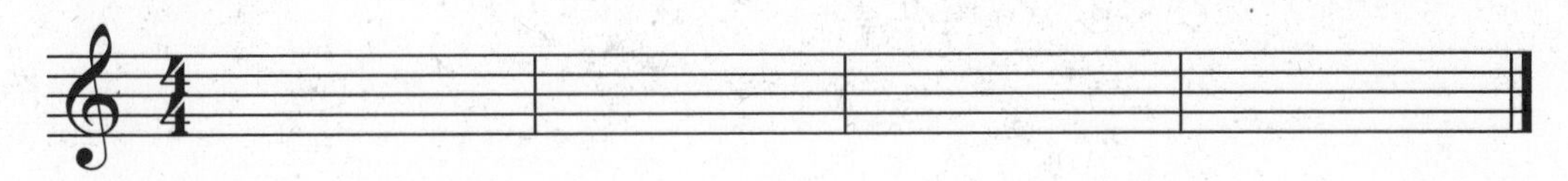

Pitches: E G A B

Using Recorder Master R•2

Objectives

- Students will review playing B A G.
- Students will learn to play E.
- Students will use all four pitches in playing short pieces.
- Students will compose a B A G E piece.

Preparation

- Have students review posture, holding position, and fingering for B A G.
- Explain procedure for three-part echoing:
  1. Listen to phrase to be echoed.
  2. Sing pitch names and finger silently.
  3. Play echo.
- Review "holding position"—recorder in position, mouthpiece on chin—while listening to instructions.

Procedure

- Have students echo short B A G phrases.
- Demonstrate fingering for E and have students finger silently back and forth between G and E, then finger silently B A G E.
- Have students perform three-part echoes on your B A G E phrases; emphasize G E and E G.
- Have students practice B A G E echoes with a partner.
- Have students read and sing the pitch names of the two pieces on Recorder Master R•2 and finger the notes silently on their recorders.
- Have students work alone or with a partner to compose and notate their own B A G E pieces.

Name ______________________________ Date ______________

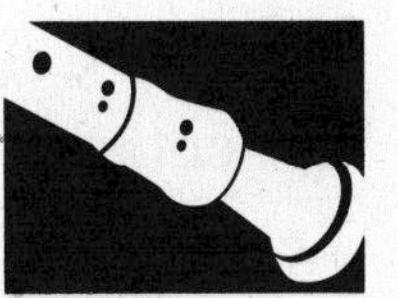

Three and Three

Today we will learn the next note in our downward sequence: B A G E and now D. We'll skip F for now. As we add D, we discover that we have all the notes to play the entire pentatonic scale with G as *do.*

- Sit up tall, hold your recorder in proper playing position, left hand fingers ready to play G, right hand thumb supporting the instrument. Play and hold for four beats G; then play and hold E for four beats. Now cover the next hole down with your right hand ring finger, and play and hold that D for four beats. Three left hand fingers, three right hand fingers.
- In quartets, see how many different arrangements of G E D you can come up with—G E D, D E G, D G E, etc. When each of the four of you has a different arrangement of these three notes, share them with the class.

"In That Great Git'n Up Mornin'" is also a song built on a pentatonic scale. When *do* is on C, the pentatonic scale looks like this.

- Name the notes in the C pentatonic scale that you can play on your recorder. Play the notes you know: start at A and go down slowly. When you come to the note you do not know on your recorder, sing its name.
- Even without that valuable *do,* we have enough notes in the C pentatonic scale for a playalong with "In That Great Git'n Up Mornin'." Try first playing just the responses on the words *fare-thee-well*, the first one with the same notes as the tune, the second one a countermelody.

Pitches: D E G A B

Using Recorder Master R•3

Objectives

- Students will review E and learn how to play D on the recorder and in small groups improvise phrases with different placements of G E D.
- Students will demonstrate knowledge of notes they can play in C pentatonic (D E G A) and perform them in playalongs to "In That Great Git'n Up Mornin'."

Preparation

- Have displayed on the chalkboard the G and C pentatonic scales with syllable names written below them. Even though these are shown on Recorder Master R•3, it can be a clearer explanation to students if all direct their attention at first to this chart.
- Lead students to discovery of difference and sameness in the two scales:

  G pentatonic here starts with *so la* before coming to *do*.

  Both have the same five syllables, but on different pitches.
- Have students identify the notes that are in both scales and tell which notes they know how to play on the recorder. (D E G A in both; can play E G A.)

Procedure

- Have students echo patterns on E G A using three-part echo system. Let them take turns being the echo leader.
- After they have participated in the above attention to the C and G pentatonic scales, have them show a partner on their own Recorder Master the common notes in both scales.
- Demonstrate placing three right hand fingers on the lower notes, left hand still in G position, thus producing D. Be careful to cover both holes completely.
- Have students practice several times, slowly, going back and forth between G and D. Be sure they place all three fingers down at the same time, not one by one.
- Have students play, 4 beats each, G E D, then D E G. Repeat this several times.
- Point out that D is another note in both C and G pentatonic scales. It completes the G pentatonic (D E G A B) and leaves out only the home tone (C) in C pentatonic.
- After they know "In That Great Git'n Up Mornin'," divide class, half singing the first part of the phrases, half singing *fare-thee-well*. Change parts.
- Have students sing pitch names for the words *fare-thee-well*. Change parts.
- Have students sing playalong on *fare-thee-well*, then combine sung playalong with song and Orff playalong on page 13 of student book.

Name ______________________ Date ______________

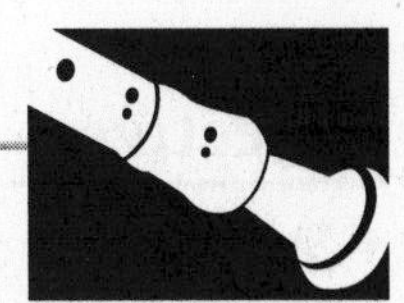

Fill in the Blanks

In this lesson you are Composer-of-the-Day. Just like any other composer—Mozart or Beethoven or Springsteen, for instance—you will need to build on the knowledge you already have. Let's review the things you know that you can use in your composition:

You can read, write, sing, and play the notes of the pentatonic scale when *do,* the home tone or tonal center, is on G.

You can read, write, and perform notes of many different time values.

You know that phrases can be alike, somewhat alike, or different.

- Knowing these things, finish the composition in the measures below:

Choose whether the fourth phrase should be A', B' or something entirely different like C.

Discuss with a partner the form you have chosen.

Play your piece for the class.

End your piece on G or B.

- Practice the playalong below. Perform it with "Amazing Grace."

Pitches: *D E G A B*

Using Recorder Master R • 4

Objectives

- Students will complete a four-phrase composition using notes of the G pentatonic scale.
- Students will perform a playalong with "Amazing Grace."

Preparation

- Discuss the process of composing music. Have students name composers they have heard of.
- Guide students to awareness of their familiarity with the G pentatonic.
- Give students various rhythm patterns in G pentatonic to echo. Review three-part echo.

Procedure

- Have students play echoes in pairs to be sure all are able to play the G pentatonic tones.
- Have students clap and speak pitch names for phrase A in piece to be completed.
- Have students sing pitch names, fingering the notes silently.
- Have students play phrase A.
- Discuss form and the form possibilities for completing the composition.
- Have students analyze and discuss the different ways the student composers have chosen to solve the composition problem.
- Have a few students teach their composition to the class.
- Have students pat the rhythm of the playalong as they speak the pitch names.
- Have students sing the pitch names as they finger their recorder silently.
- Perform the playalong as written.
- Perform "Amazing Grace" with the playalong in a variety of ways, such as half the class singing while the other half plays the recorder; playalong with recordings.
- This could be an appropriate and effective large performance piece with singers, recorder players, and Orff instruments.
- Demonstrate fingering for D' (left middle finger only, no thumb).
- Encourage students to play the melody of "Amazing Grace."

Name ______________________ Date ______________

From C to C'

It's time to add C in two octaves (C and C'), and its upper neighbor D'.

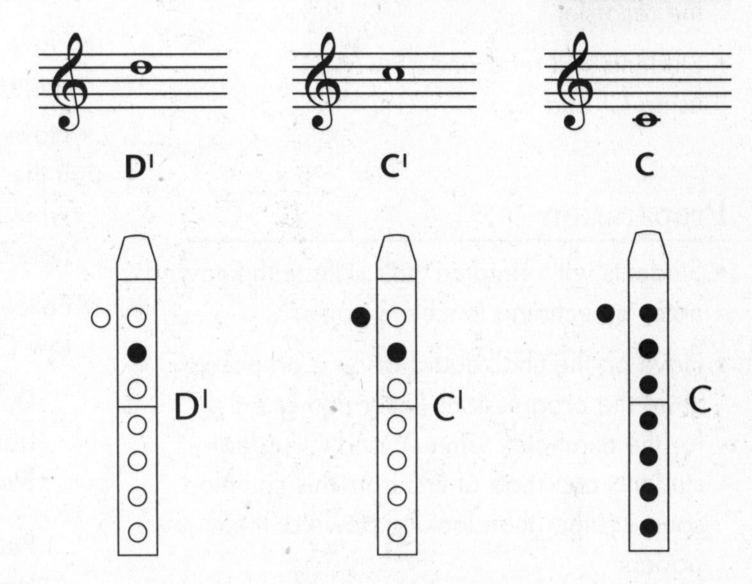

- Let's start with D'. With your recorder in playing position, cover the second hole with your left middle finger, remove your thumb, and you have high D, or D'.
- First finger silently, then play D' to D and back again, slowly. As you can see, this octave requires one finger only for its higher note but three fingers from each hand and a thumb for its lower note. Be sure to cover all the needed holes at one time, no peeling down one by one.
- Now for C'. From D', played with middle finger only, without thumb hole covered, simply cover the thumb hole. Keep the middle finger where it is.
- Read "Nani Wala Na Hala." First clap the rhythm and say the pitch names, then sing the pitch names and finger the notes silently. Finally play the melody.
- Low C. All the holes are covered. All the right hand fingers are used. Blow very gently. It is easier to learn this note by stepping down to it:

G – E – D – C   A – G – E – D – C   C' – A – G – E – D – C

Notice that each of the bottom two notes of the recorder has two holes instead of one. Be very careful to cover them completely. Finger and sing, then play these progressions down, then back up, several times.

- Read "Fun wa ni alaafia." Clap the rhythm and say the pitch names. Sing the pitch names and finger the notes silently. Now play the song slowly. After playing the song together several times, try variations.

Pitches: C D E G A B C' D'

Using Recorder Master R•5

Objectives

- Students will learn to play D^I, C^I and C on the recorder.
- Students will read and play two pieces using C^I and C.

Preparation

- Students will reinforce their skills with known notes by echoing teacher's patterns.
- Have on the chalkboard or on a prepared chart the progressions (letter names only) for the examples using D^I and C^I so that students can read at first from this common source rather than looking down at their papers.

  D^I-C^I-D^I

  D^I-C^I-A

  D^I-C^I-G

  D^I-C^I-A-G

  D^I-C^I-A-G-E

  D^I-C^I-A-G-E-D

- Make the same preparation for the progressions using C^I and C.

Procedure

- Demonstrate fingering for high D (D^I). Caution students about overblowing this note especially.
- The challenge on Recorder Master R•5 is very difficult. Have students try it, but do not dwell on it in this lesson.
- Demonstrate fingering for high C (C^I), then for moving between D^I and C^I.
- Have students read from the board or chart, finger silently, then play the first set of progressions listed on R•5.
- Have students read, clap, and sing pitch names (and/or syllable names) for "Nani Wala Na Hala" (student book p. 276).
- Have students sing pitch names again while fingering notes on their recorders.
- Have students play "Nani Wala Na Hala." If the difficulty is too great for playing the whole piece, have them play only the first note of each measure with the recording.
- Follow above procedure for introducing low C:

  Demonstrate fingering, cautioning about covering all the holes and blowing very gently.

  Read and play appropriate progressions from the board or chart.

- Remind students, as often as necessary, about covering the holes completely. This is much harder on the lower notes, especially the double holes for D and C. Help students adjust the foot piece to fit their hands. It is often the sixth hole (played with weaker ring finger) that is the culprit in an air-leak caused by a hole not completely covered.
- Have students read, clap and say pitch names for "Fun wa ni alaafia" (student book p. 248).
- Have students finger silently, then play the song.
- Have students try these variations.

1. One group plays the first and third measures; another group plays the second and fourth measures (call and response).
2. Divide into four groups, standing in square formation. Each group plays one measure.
3. Make two circles. Inner circle plays the song, outer circle performs the movement suggested. Change parts.

Name ______________________ Date ______________

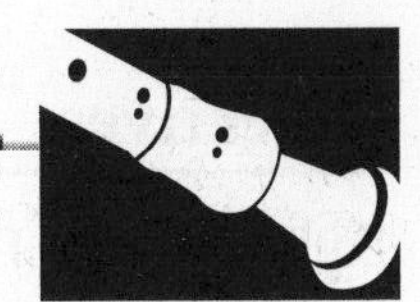

Fitting Pieces Together

Today we will add new parts to the beautiful Korean song "Arirang."

- First, be sure you can sing it in its simplest, most straightforward form.
- Study the playalong below. Sing the pitches and finger them silently. Notice the form of the playalong: A B C B. What are the signs that tell you this? Now play it.

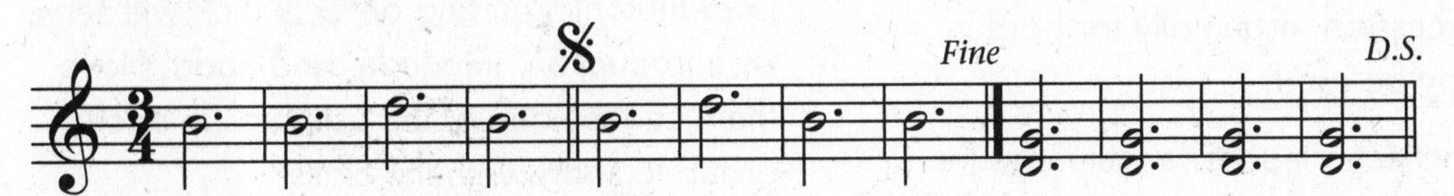

- Find the $\frac{3}{4}$ percussion ostinato you created in Lesson 1. In groups of 4 each plays his or her ostinato while the other three sing the song. Choose one of the four that seems to go best with "Arirang."
- In the same groups of 4, improvise four measures in G pentatonic which can be used as an introduction, an interlude between verses, and a coda at the end of the song. Make your improvisation end on G. Choose one from your group and notate it below:

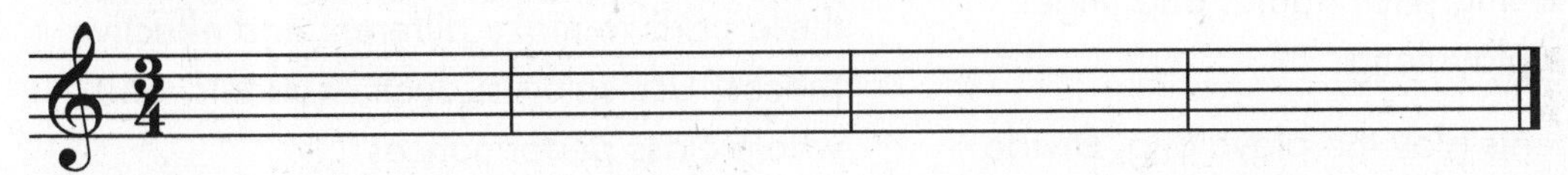

- Combine these parts in your group of 4 and perform them as the class sings: Improvisation, Bordun of G and D played on the first beat of each measure, and Percussion ostinato.

Pitches: D E G A B D'

Using Recorder Master R•6

Objectives

- Students will perform a playalong with "Arirang."
- Students will improvise short phrases in the G pentatonic scale to serve as introduction, interludes, and coda to "Arirang."

Preparation

- Melodic percussion, especially for bordun G and D may be used.
- Have students echo teacher's four-measure phrases in G pentatonic, triple meter.
- Have students sing "Arirang," as it appears on page 50 in the student book.

Procedure

- Have students analyze the playalong, telling how the signs explain it's A B C B form.
- Have students sing pitch names and finger silently on the playalong.
- Have all students play the playalong. Divide on phrase C so that some are playing G and others are playing D. Then divide the class and have half play the playalong and half sing "Arirang." Exchange parts.
- Have students review the triple-meter percussion ostinatos they created in Lesson 1.
- Divide class into groups of 4 and have groups play their ostinatos with the song. Then have them choose one ostinato in each group to perform for the class.
- Have students in the same groups of 4 improvise a four-measure piece in G pentatonic, ending on G, which will serve as introduction, interlude, and coda. Have them choose one of the ostinatos in each group to share with the class.
- Have students in each group notate their chosen improvisation.
- Have groups combine their chosen percussion ostinato, improvisation, and a bordun of G and D to perform for the class.
- Have students combine various parts into a whole to go with "Arirang." Have them experiment with different ways of combining these parts to make different and effective pieces. Use soloists, duets, quartets, and whole class performances.

Name ______________________ Date ____________

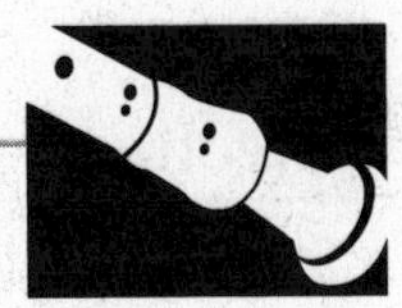

Closing That Gap

You know now all the notes you need to play the C and G pentatonic scales, both of which contain the tone syllables *do, re, mi, so,* and *la.*

If you spell out these two scales together, C D E G A B, only one pitch name is missing: F. It's time now to fill in that gap.

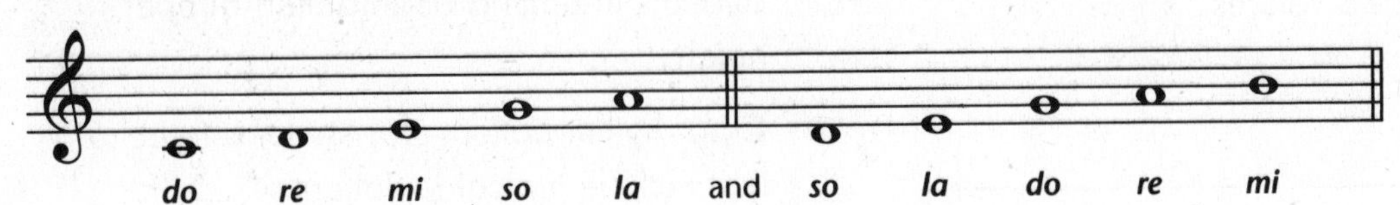

F

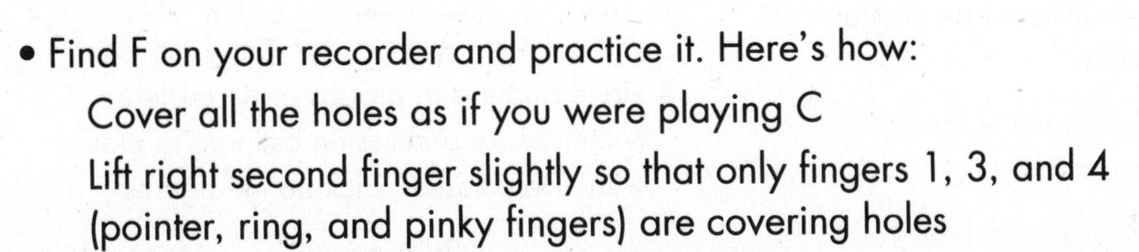

- Find F on your recorder and practice it. Here's how:

  Cover all the holes as if you were playing C

  Lift right second finger slightly so that only fingers 1, 3, and 4 (pointer, ring, and pinky fingers) are covering holes

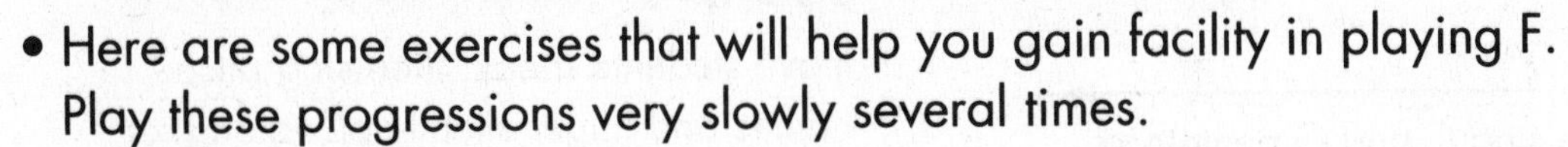

- Here are some exercises that will help you gain facility in playing F. Play these progressions very slowly several times.

  C – F F – C G – F F – G G – F – E E – F– G

- In groups of 4 create a two-measure percussion ostinato. Have each group perform its ostinato while the rest of the class sings "De colores."
- First speak, then sing pitch names and finger silently the playalong.

Pitches: *C D E F G A*

Using Recorder Master R•7

Objectives

- Students will learn to play F on their recorders.
- Students will create a percussion accompaniment to emphasize the $\frac{6}{8}$ meter of "De colores" and combine it with the song and the playalong.
- Students will learn a counter-melody playalong to "De colores."

Preparation

- Have a variety of non-tuned percussion instruments available.
- Display C and G pentatonic scales on chalkboard or on a chart.

Procedure

- Have students sing C and G pentatonic scales with tone syllables.
- Guide students in spelling the pitch names of the two scales together and to the discovery that F is not present in either scale.
- Have students start at C^1 and play all the notes they know in descending order: C^1 B A G E D C.
- Demonstrate F on the recorder, showing fingering relationship between F and C.
- Have students practice progressions including F as listed in Recorder Master R•7.
- Have students sing "De colores," leading students in patting beat (dotted quarter note).
- Clap rhythm patterns for students to echo that include typical $\frac{6}{8}$ patterns

- Have students in groups of 4 create a two-measure percussion ostinato to play with "De colores." Include the figures and .
- Have students speak, then sing pitch names and finger silently playalong for "De colores."
- Have students perform playalong.
- Have students combine percussion ostinato and playalong with song, with or without recording.

Name ______________________ Date ____________

Playing Together

Today we will learn to play in duet a famous melody by Beethoven, called here "Ode to Joy," and taken from his Ninth Symphony.

First let's discuss four ways in which two melodies can be played together.

Unison—in which both melodies play the same note, sometimes an octave apart

Parallel motion—in which both melodies move mostly in the same direction

Contrary motion—in which the melodies move mostly in opposite directions

Oblique motion—in which one voice moves while the other is relatively static

- Sing and play these examples:

- Here is "Ode to Joy" arranged as a duet. What kinds of melodic motion do you find in it?

Pitches: C D E F G A B C' D'

Using Recorder Master R•8

Objectives

- Students will distinguish differences in parallel, contrary and oblique motion and play patterns in each type.
- Students will learn to play "Ode to Joy" in two parts.

Preparation

- Students will need additional practice on the difficult new notes, especially C and F, which will be used in this lesson. Be sure to demonstrate again how to finger C and F.
- Give students melodic patterns to echo which include C and F in stepwise progression; e.g., G F G; G F E; F E F; D F E; E D C; C D E F; etc.

Procedure

- Have students tell definitions of the different types of melodic movement.
- Have students draw in the air and on the chalkboard illustrations of parallel, contrary and oblique motion.
- Have students sing the thirds in the example of parallel motion. Sing pitch names and finger silently. Play the example.
- Have students sing the parts separately, then together in the example of contrary motion. Sing pitch names and finger silently. Play the example.
- Have students sing the parts separately, then together in the example of oblique motion. Sing pitch names and finger silently. Play the example.
- Have pairs of students devise movement to illustrate these three types of melodic motion.
- Have students sing "Ode to Joy" as it appears on page 103 in the student book, then sing pitch names of the melody on Recorder Master.
- Have all students play melody of "Ode to Joy."
- Divide the class and have students play the duet arrangement of "Ode to Joy."

Name ______________________ Date ______________

Dig-a-dig-a-doo

- Remember how hard it is to say tongue twisters—several times and in a hurry! Try saying, "Peter Piper picked a peck of pickled peppers" or "How can a clam cram in a clean cream can?"

You are used to producing your recorder tones by blowing a gentle, whispered *doo*. This is the articulation used most often. But what happens when you play a succession of fast notes?

- Try this pattern first by *speaking doo.* It gets pretty hard! You're very glad for that 8th rest in the middle! Now try speaking this: *dig-a-doo, dig-a-dig-a-dig-a-dig-a-dig-a* (clap) *dig-a-doo, dig-a-dig-a-dig-a-dig-a* (clap). Easier? That's because your tongue is getting tiny rests from saying the very same sound over and over very quickly. Now play this pattern on your recorder using the *dig-a-dig-a* articulation. Leave out the claps; just think them silently.
- Here is a playalong for "Joshua Fit the Battle of Jericho."

* woodblock

Pitches: D E F G A

Using Recorder Master R • 9

Objectives

- Students will learn articulation for series of sixteenth notes.
- Students will perform playalong with "Joshua Fit the Battle of Jericho."

Preparation

- Review "doo" articulation in series of patterns for students to echo.
- Play D F A and A G F E D slowly for students to echo.

Procedure

- Define *articulation* (sometimes referred to as *tonguing*): the manner in which separate notes are joined to each other. The way tones are begun and ended is very important in recorder articulation. So far students have worked for smooth tonguing, produced by a whispered *doo* and ended with a light *t*, or simply by placing the tip of the tongue against the roof of the mouth. Now they will learn a new articulation produced by *dig-a-dig-a* for a series of sixteenth notes.
- Have students echo short phrases within the pitch range of D-A, practicing different articulations:

  smooth (legato)—*doo–t* for the time value of the note

  detached (staccato)—*doo-t* quickly

  series of short notes—*dig-a-dig-a*
- Have different students read the tongue twisters. Have them tell why they are difficult to say quickly and repeatedly (similar word beginning sounds).
- Have students play the exercise with *doo* articulation, then with *dig-a-dig-a*. Have them describe the difference.
- Have students speak the articulation (doo and *dig-a*) in the playalong for "Joshua Fit the Battle of Jericho," clapping at the suggested places.
- Have students finger the notes and whisper the articulation in the playalong, then play it.
- Divide the class, half playing the playalong while the other half sings. Have a volunteer play the woodblock on the suggested places.

Name ______________________ Date ____________

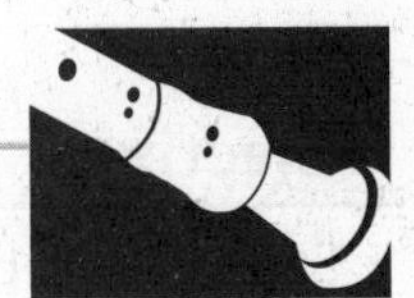

Turn, Turn . . . Come Round Right

Let's start by making sure everybody can do four things with the song "Simple Gifts."

- First, sing the song as it appears on page 136 in your book.
- Next, try this easy playalong. Since the song is built on only two chords and one note occurs in both of them, that one common tone can be used to accompany the song throughout.

- Now play the four-beat percussion ostinato you composed in an earlier lesson. Practice it a time or two, then let a few volunteers play their ostinatos while the rest of the class performs the song and playalong.
- The last part is the simple movement pattern outlined in your book. Review it with your teacher, then dance it with the recording.
- Let's put it all together, playing in four groups, each with a different activity. Follow the teacher's directions.

You can do all those things separately; now let's see if you can play and move at the same time!

- Learn this round by rote, phrase by phrase.

- Follow the teacher's directions for movement to the round.

Pitches: D E G A B D'

Using Recorder Master R • 10

Objectives

- Students will perform "Simple Gifts" in four ways: song, playalong, percussion ostinato, movement.
- Students will learn a round by rote, movement for the round, then perform movement and music together.

Preparation

- Students will have learned to sing "Simple Gifts."
- Remind students to recall the percussion ostinatos they created and notated in Teacher's Resource Master R•7 (p. 117).

Procedure

(Note to Teacher: This lesson may be too long to complete in one session. If so, review and continue in the next class.)

- Have students sing "Simple Gifts."
- Explain to students that D is a note common to both the chords needed for the melody of "Simple Gifts" and can therefore be used throughout the song.
- Have students play the playalong to "Simple Gifts."
- Have students practice their own ostinatos, then have a few volunteers play them.
- Have students review the dance steps in the text, then dance to the recording.
- Use this sequence for students to play in groups.

1. Divide the class into four groups. Each group will perform all four activities. Assign a station, a place for each part to be performed—instruments together for percussion ostinato, space for movement, singers, and recorder players.
2. Have each group decide on one percussion ostinato to be used for its turn with the ostinato; be sure the whole group participates in it.
3. Group 1 begins with the song; group 2 with the playalong; group 3 with the percussion ostinato; group 4 with the movement.
4. At the end of the first performance, each group moves quietly and quickly—in 8 beats—to the next station and the piece is performed again.
5. Repeat this process until all four groups have performed all four activities.

- Each group will perform each activity, moving quickly from one place to another at the conclusion of each activity.
- Teach the round by rote, phrase by phrase, using the three-part echo system. When they can play it comfortably in unison, have students play in a two-part, then a four-part round.
- Teach the simple movement steps and have them perform them. In random space, have students perform each of the following in eight beats:

  1. 3 steps forward, close;
  2. 3 steps back, close;
  3. 4 "tip-taps" (step-close-step) in place;
  4. individual circle in place, close.

- Have students perform these steps in unison, then in a round, first two parts, then four parts. When they are comfortable with the movement progression, have them play the round as they move the parts.
- With the four groups in a square, have them perform the round with the movement.

Name ______________________________ Date ______________

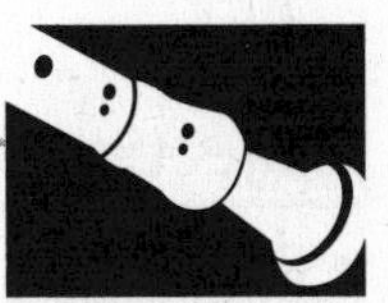

Mood Music

- After you have learned to sing "Kojo No Tsuki," try playing it with this playalong.

- What note do you play many times? Would you be able to play the entire tune on your recorder? Why or why not?
- What adjectives would you use to describe this tune?

In the 1600s a special poetic form began to develop in Japan. It was always short, descriptive, fit into a specific number of syllables, and almost always about something to make people feel connected to nature. It usually describes an event of one single moment. It was called *haiku*. Since its Japanese beginning nearly four hundred years ago, haiku has become popular all over the world.

The traditional form of haiku is three lines, seventeen syllables: five in the first line, seven in the second, and five in the third line, and is often written to look like this:

_____ _____ _____ _____ _____

_____ _____ _____ _____ _____ _____ _____

_____ _____ _____ _____ _____

Here are examples (available on the Internet) written by fifth and sixth grade students:

A heron rises
In the middle of the swamp
Under the full moon.

A little girl stands
Holding her finger out and
A butterfly comes.

- Now it's your turn to write a haiku.

Pitches: *E A B C'*

Using Recorder Master R • 11

Objectives

- Students will perform a playalong with "Kojo No Tsuki."
- Students will write examples of haiku.
- Students will combine their haiku, the song, and the playalong.

Preparation

- Students will be able to sing "Kojo No Tsuki."
- Lead students in a discussion on the mood of the song—thoughtful, reflective, serious. Ask for their words of description.
- Play the playalong, first all together, then half the class playing while the other half sings; change parts.
- Ask students why they would be unable to play this entire song on their recorders *(notes lower than the instrument can play)*.
- Lead students through the information about haiku, and guide them in finding suitable subjects for their own creative writing.
- Have students read aloud the examples of haiku. Show them how certain words, or whole lines can be extended or repeated to enhance the meaning.
- Prepare students to write their own haiku. Begin by having students listen again to the recording of "Kojo No Tsuki."
- Say to students: "Think of a subject related to nature—a season of the year, the moon, a rose, a sparkling stream, or any one of dozens of other things, something meaningful to you. Now read the haiku examples and determine if they fall into this description of the haiku form above. Think of a single thing in your own experience and create your haiku."
- Have students write individual haiku.
- Divide the class into groups of four who will share their performances with the entire class, reading haiku with the song as a background enhancement of the mood. Suggest that students read haiku slowly and consider using appropriate pauses.

Name ______________________ Date ______________

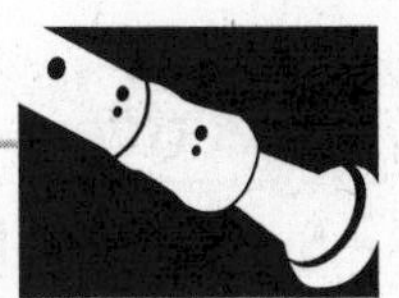

The Backbone of Harmony

You have learned that any two or more pitches sounded together make harmony. However, harmony is also a system of chords. Today we will experience the two most important chords in any key: the tonic and the dominant chords.

Once you know the formula for making these chords, you can build them in every key.

First you need to know that they are built on thirds, and when they are complete they have three tones and are called triads. You can see their structure more clearly on a keyboard.

- Here are the tonic and dominant triads (chords), the tonic, starting on the first tone of the key, is built on steps 1, 3, and 5 or in this case C, E, and G. They are usually identified by their Roman numeral names: tonic = I; dominant = V.

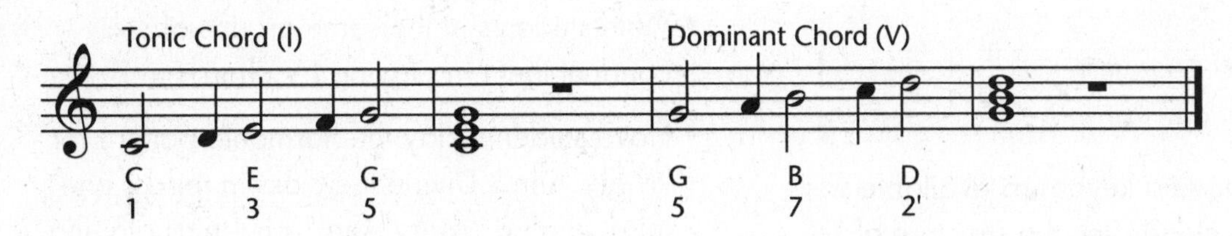

- Play slowly the three notes of each of these chords, then divide into groups of six. Then play the chords in these patterns:

I I V V I   I V I V I   I V V V I

- Listen for the song the teacher has played for you. Try it in the key of F with these chords.

- Here is the harmonic pattern for "Mary Ann" and a plan for performing it:

F F C C   C C F F   F F C C   C C F F (all whole notes)

Pitches: C E F G A B C D'

Using Recorder Master R • 12

Objectives

- Students will learn about tonic and dominant chords and to play in harmony the tones that make up these chords in C and F.
- Students will accompany a familiar song they hear with tonic (I) and dominant (V) chords in C and the song, "Mary Ann" in F.

Preparation

- Prepare a staff on a chalkboard or chart with notes for the I and V chords written out in C. Prepare a second chart with notes for the I and V chords for F.
- Be ready to play on keyboard or to sing "Clementine" for students to identify and accompany with I and V chords.

- If possible, have a keyboard available so students can clearly see the structure of triadic chords.

Procedure

- Guide students in a discussion on harmony, the sounding of pitches together, leading into tonic and dominant chords as the most important and frequently-used chords in our music.
- Show students on the prepared chart how the tonic and dominant chords in C are made; then show them on a keyboard. This will show more clearly the thirds on which they are built.
- Have students play slowly the notes for the two chords: C E G and G B D.
- Divide the class into groups of six, assigning each student a particular tone: C E G G B D[I]. Note that G appears twice, so two students will be assigned that note.
- Indicate when each chord is to be played—by holding up one finger or 5, for instance—then conduct the class in playing a series of I-V chords in C.
- Play "Clementine" and ask if they recognize it. Then ask students to indicate by holding up one or five fingers which chord should be played as you play the song again.
- Have students play I and V chords appropriately as you play "Clementine."
- Show on chart I and V chords in F and have students play slowly the notes: F A C and C E G, again noting that the two chords have one note in common.
- With students in the same groups of six, conduct them in playing I V chords in F.
- Have students play the harmonic pattern for "Mary Ann." Divide the class in thirds, one third singing "Mary Ann," one third playing F chords, and one third playing C chords (assign notes to individuals). Switch parts so that all sing, play tonic chords, play dominant chords.
- Refer to "Mary Ann" in Orff Orchestrations 5, page 51. Incorporate the recorder chords with the Orff instruments.
- Have some students singing "Mary Ann," some playing F chords (I) when they are appropriate, and some playing C chords (V) when appropriate.
- It is likely that some students will immediately notice that the tonic in C is the same as the dominant in F.

Name ______________________ Date ______________

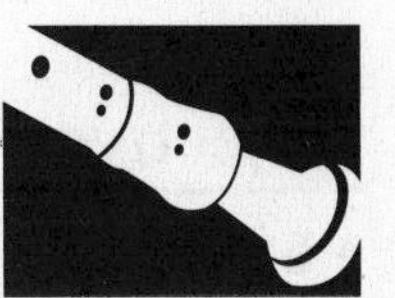

Roots, Inversions, and Another Triad

It's easy to remember—because of the word *triad*—that chords are basically made of *three* tones, the *root* which is the foundation of the triad and the tone that gives it its name; the *third* above the root; and the *fifth* above the root. The two main chords are: tonic (I) and dominant (V).

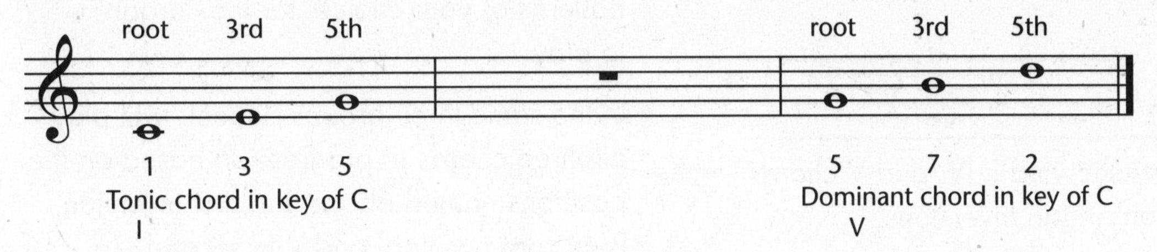

It's time to add another triad, this time the subdominant. As *sub* means *down* or *under*, you'll not be surprised to discover that the subdominant is just below the dominant, its root being the 4th step of the scale.

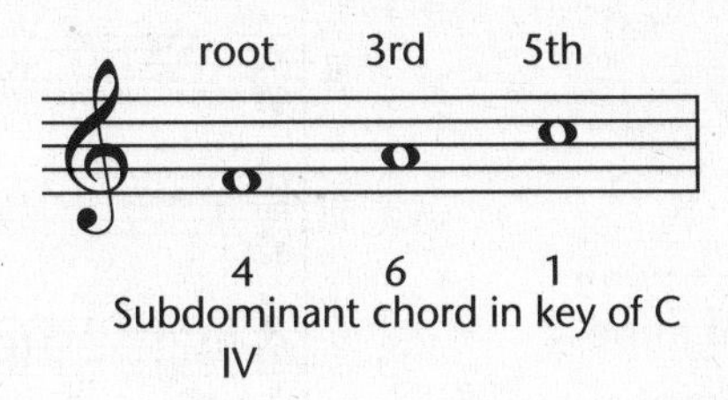

These three triads are in root position as you see them here: their roots are their lowest tones. In the case of both the IV and the V chords, root position makes the chord 5ths go into the next higher octave. There are other possibilities. What if you inverted the triads, turned them upside down?

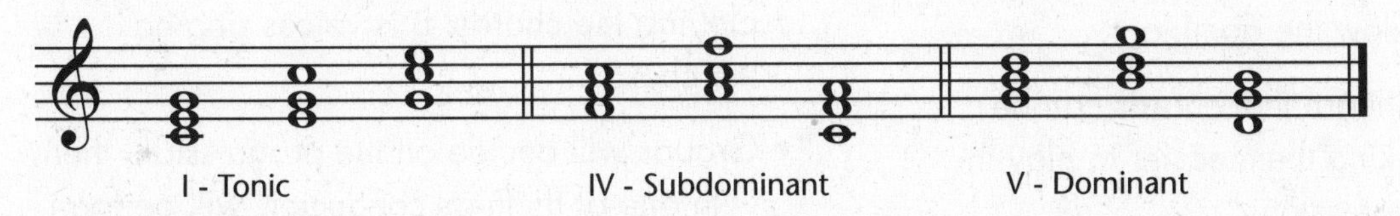

Look carefully at the notes. Which version of the tonic chord is easier to play on the recorder? The subdominant? The dominant? Notice that some are much easier to play on the recorder than others.

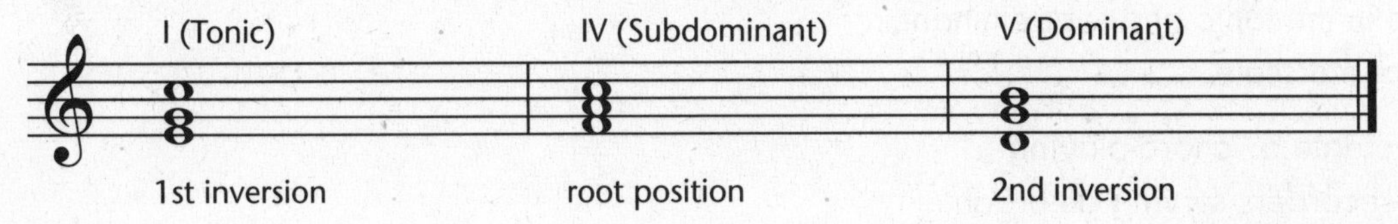

Pitches: D E F G A B C'

Using Recorder Master R • 13

Objectives

- Students will learn that triads are chords of three members, root, third, and fifth.
- Students will learn that the subdominant is also one of the primary chords.
- Students will play I, IV, and V chords in root position and in inversions.

Preparation

- Prepare charts showing I, IV, and V chords in root position and in inversions.
- Write these progressions on the chalkboard for students to follow:

  I – IV – V – I

  I – V – I – IV – V – I

Procedure

- Students will define a triad chord of three tones, the root, the third above the root, and the fifth above the root.
- Students will see, preferably on a keyboard, that triads in root position are built on thirds.
- Students will define a subdominant chord as the chord below the dominant.
- Students will learn that chords can be inverted, making them easier to play in recorder progressions.
- Students will tell that there is a common tone in tonic and dominant chords, the fifth of the scale, and they will learn there is also a common tone in the tonic and subdominant, the first step of the scale.
- Students will create a "chord-playing organ," with recorders serving as organ pipes in the key of C. Students will form three groups: a tonic chord first inversion: E G C'; a dominant chord second inversion: D G B; and a subdominant chord root position: F A C'.
- Within each group each student will be assigned a specific note of the chord.
- Conduct the chord patterns, or random patterns of your choice, for the "organ" to play.
- In the same three groups students will play all three chords in progression based on the positions named above: I in first inversion, IV in root position, and V in second inversion.

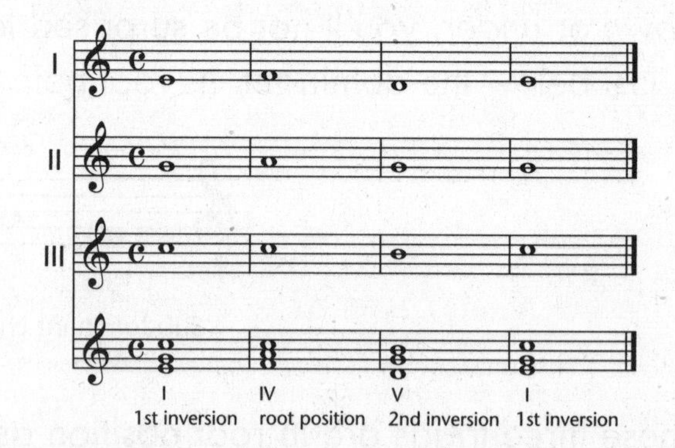

- Conduct students in chord progressions.
- Have students in the three groups make an ABA chordal composition: A is recorders playing the chords, B is voices singing the chords.
- Groups will decide on the progression, then, with one of them as conductor, will perform their composition for the class.

Name ______________________ Date ______________

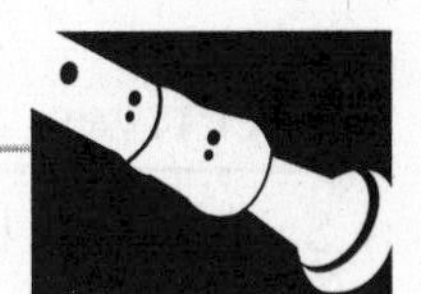

Incomplete Triads

You've learned a lot about chords. Today you will see that even an incomplete chord can make clear whether it is tonic, subdominant, or dominant. Usually such a partial chord will include the root and often its 3rd, but the root and the 5th are sometimes used as well, and occasionally the root alone will be used to identify the chord.

- You have sung "Cuando salí de Cuba." Now perform this playalong with the recording.

- Can you tell which chords are suggested in the playalong? At the Xs write I, IV, or V where you think they are appropriate.
- Perhaps two students would like to add this part on claves:

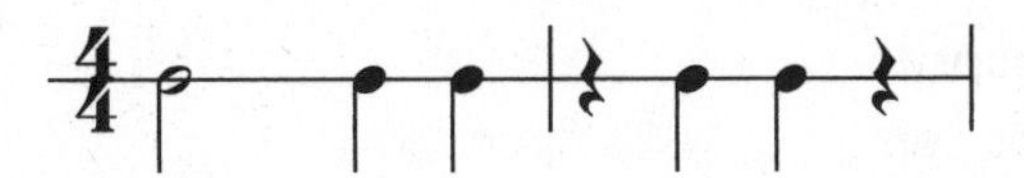

- "Tzena, Tzena" is very different from "Cuando salí de Cuba" in many ways—one song comes from Israel, the other from Cuba; one is fast and carefree, the other is more thoughtful and serious. Yet both songs use the same chords!
- Here is the chord pattern, one chord per measure of 4 beats: **C F G C** repeated throughout the piece.
- That's too easy; let's add a small challenge:

  Use the same pattern, but play various notes within each chord—any tone you choose so long as it is within the appropriate chord.

  Let's review the chords: C (I) = C, E and G
F (IV) = F, A and C
G (V) = G, B and D

Pitches: C D E F G A B C' D'

Using Recorder Master R • 14

Objectives

- Students will learn that incomplete primary chords can be identified as I, IV, or V chords.
- Students will perform a playalong with "Cuando salí de Cuba."
- Students will identify the chord pattern for "Tzena Tzena" and play tones from each of the chords to accompany the song.

Preparation

- Students will have learned "Cuando salí de Cuba" and "Tzena Tzena."

Procedure

- Students will review their knowledge of chords: composed of root, 3rd and 5th; can be inverted; can be sounded together or separately; can have a common note with another chord.
- Students will work in small groups to discover that incomplete chords can also indicate chordal identity.
- Students will play the playalong with "Cuando salí de Cuba."
- Students will study the playalong for "Cuando salí de Cuba" and write in the chord names where they are called for.
- Students will perform the playalong for "Cuando salí de Cuba" again, with two students playing the claves part.
- Students will discover the chord pattern for "Tzena Tzena" is C F G C repeated throughout the piece and choose tones from these chords and play them as a practice exercise.
- Students will decide which notes they will play for each chord, then play the chords together.
- Students will divide so that half the class sings "Tzena Tzena" and half plays recorders on the accompanying chords.
- Finally all students will play chords to accompany the recording.

Name ______________________________ Date ______________

Sharp That F

We have talked often about the key of G, and played pieces and playalongs and descants in G. But we've never been able to spell out and play the three primary chords in G . . . because we need one more note we haven't yet learned to play: F-sharp. Here is the G major scale, the three primary chords, and the way to finger F#.

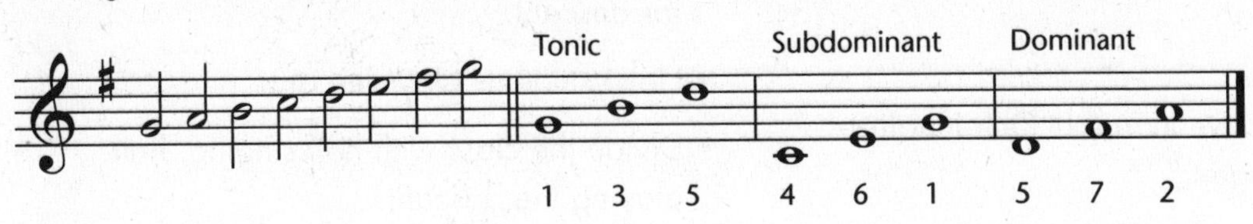

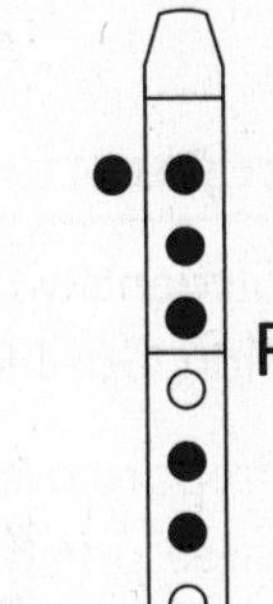

- This is not a hard note to play. First get your G fingering, place your right hand very near the holes for the lower notes, then cover the holes with right fingers 2 and 3. Now try these progressions:

G – F# – G
G – F# – D – G
G – F# – D – F# – G
G – F# – E – F# – G

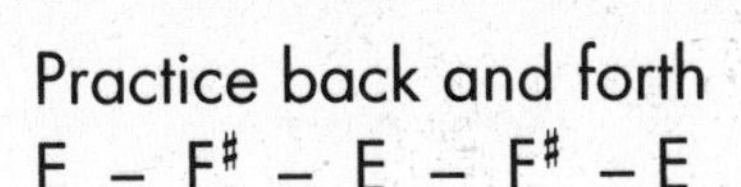
Practice back and forth
E – F# – E – F# – E

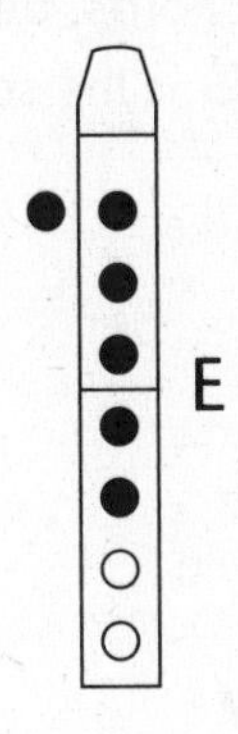

- Sing "Och Jungfrau Hon Går I Ringen" again, and as you sing, feel the swing of the triple meter. Next, read the notes from your book and play the song on your recorder. They are all familiar notes except the new F#.

Pitches: D E F# G A B C D'

Using Recorder Master R • 15

Objectives

- Students will learn to play F-sharp on the recorder.
- Students will recognize the three primary chords in G.
- Students will learn a descant for "Och Jungfrau Hon Går I Ringen."

Preparation

- Students will have learned "Och Jungfrau Hon Går I Ringen."
- Prepare a chart showing G major scale and three primary triads of G.

Procedure

- Demonstrate fingering for F-sharp.
- Point out key signature that indicates key of G major and discuss the three primary chords. Be aware that the subdominant in G is the same as the tonic in C.
- Lead students in progressions involving F-sharp.
- Have students in small groups do echo work emphasizing F-sharp.
- Have students sing "Och Jungfrau Hon Går I Ringen" while doing a step-close-pause pattern.
- Have students finger and sing pitch names for descant.
- Have students play descant.
- Divide the class with half singing, half playing the descant.
- Combine song, descant, and Orff Orchestration.

Name ______________________________ Date ________________

Recorder Master R • 16

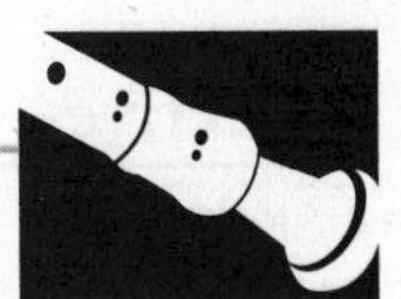

Flat That B

Just as we discovered that an F-sharp is needed for the key of G, we now must learn B-flat is needed for the key of F. Here is the F major scale, its primary chords, and a diagram for fingering B-flat.

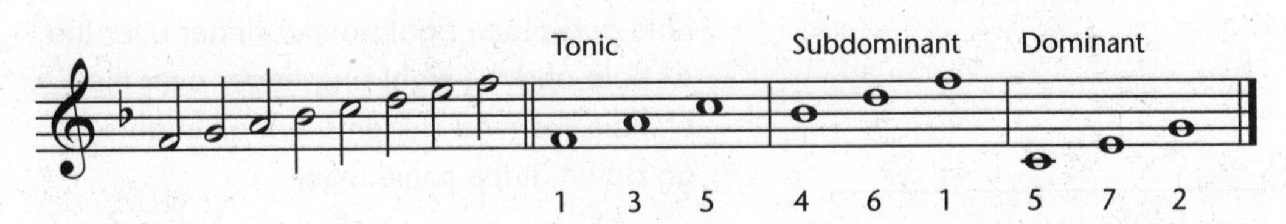

B♭

Remember that you can invert the triads, often making them easier to play.

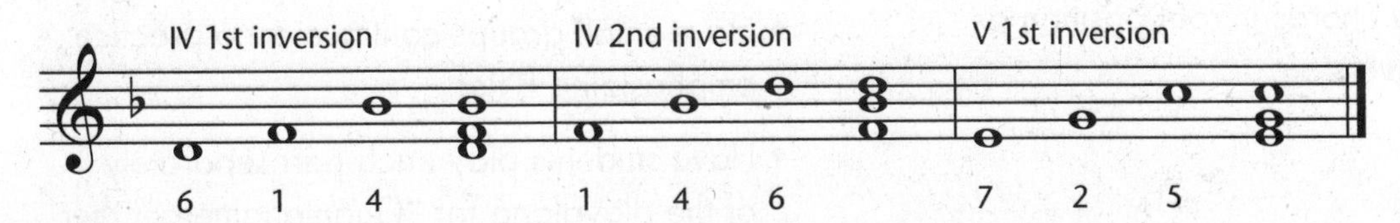

- Now for some practice on that B-flat. Practice these progressions.

  C' – B♭ – C'   B♭ – A – G   A – B♭ – C'   B♭ – G – B♭   D' – C' – B♭

- In the duet playalong below, both parts play only on the word *Guantanamera*.

Pitches: F G A B♭ C' D'

Using Recorder Master R • 16

Objectives

- Students will learn to play B-flat on the recorder.
- Students will recognize the three primary chords of F major.
- Students will perform a playalong with "Guantanamera."

Preparation

- Students will have learned to sing "Guantanamera."
- Prepare a chart showing F major scale and primary chords in root position as well as in inversion.

Procedure

- Point out key signature that indicates key of F major and discuss the three primary chords. Be aware that the dominant in F is the same as the tonic in C.
- Show inversions of chords. Explain that they often make chords easier to play, and that as long as the correct pitches are used, either octave is appropriate.
- Demonstrate fingering for B-flat. Have students begin with the G fingering, home base, lift left middle finger from the second hole and place right pointer finger over the 4th hole and the right ring finger over the 6th hole. Remind students that all fingers go down at the same time.
- Lead students in progressions involving B-flat, very slowly, feeling the fingering more than looking at it.
- Have small groups continue echo practice emphasizing B-flat.
- Have students play each part separately of the playalong for "Guantanamera," then as a duet, finally with the song and the recording. Explain to students that Part I is the melody of the song and that Part II is an accompanying melody.

Name ____________________ Date ____________

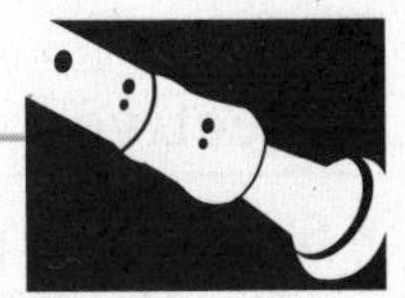

A Mixture in Blue

You can play F-sharps with no trouble, and you have played several pieces that included them. You can play B-flats with a little more trouble, but you have also played pieces that included them. Now let's see about a single piece that has not one but both of these notes and a B-natural as well!

- First try some exercises:

B – B♭ – B   B♭ – B – C' – B – B♭   B♭ – A – G   A – B♭ – A – G

- Next, play two measures from "City Blues," following teacher's instructions.
- After reading "City Blues," add this playalong:

- Add one more part: the roots of the chords for the 12-bar blues progression in the key of G.

(Reminder: I I I I IV IV I I V IV I I)

Play these chord roots with the song. Then put all the parts together.

- Write the 12-bar blues chord progression below, starting with the roots.

Pitches: D E F♯ G A B♭ B C' D'

Using Recorder Master R • 17

Objectives

- Students will perform a playalong with "City Blues" involving B-flat, B-natural, and F-sharp.
- Students will play chord roots for a 12-bar blues progression and notate its chords.

Preparation

- Students will sing the song "City Blues" and discuss what they know about blues.

Procedure

- Have students discuss the key signature and the accidentals in "City Blues."
- Have students read excerpts from "City Blues" (student book, page 278) on the recorder. Begin reading notes corresponding with the words "spent all my money on" (line 2, m. 1), and then on "really got to know your way" (line 4, m. 2).
- Remind students that when an accidental is placed before a note (in this case a flat), that accidental applies within the measure unless the sign for a *natural* occurs.
- Have the whole class read "City Blues" from the book. Next, get volunteers to play solos on lines 2 and 4 while class plays lines 1 and 3.
- Have students read playalong.
- Get volunteers for solos on lines 2 and 4; have whole class play lines 1 and 3.
- Have students add playalong to solo/chorus version of the song.
- Have students review the 12-bar blues progression and play the chord roots.
- Have students combine all these activities in performance of "City Blues": group/solo; playalong; chord roots.
- Have students work together in small groups to write the chords for the 12-bar blues progression.

Name ______________________ Date ____________

Another Note, Another Mode

The Phrygian mode is perhaps the most minor-sounding of all the modes. Play its first five tones—E to B and back down to E—and listen to its minor sound.

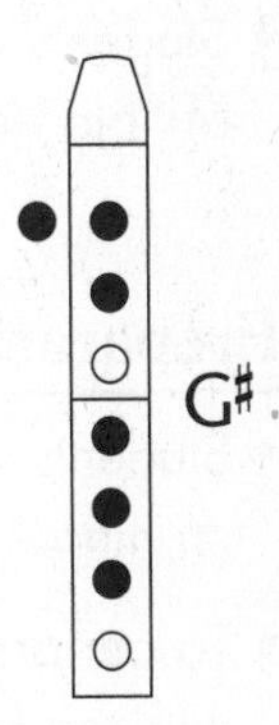

In southern Spain, the Phrygian mode is often used, but with an added G-sharp, *in addition to the G,* sometimes called the Spanish Phrygian mode. Play this from E to B and back to E. Listen to the difference.

- Practice these progressions using G#:

G – G# – G   G – G# – A   B – A – G#   E – F – G# – F – E

- Play this two-part arrangement of "No despiertes a mi niño."

Pitches: E F G G# A B C'

Using Recorder Master R • 18

Objectives

- Students will learn to play G-sharp on the recorder.
- Students will be introduced to Phrygian mode and to the "Spanish Phrygian mode," involving both a G and a G-sharp.
- Students will learn a two-part arrangement of "No despiertes a mi niño."

Preparation

- Students will have sung "No despiertes a mi niño."
- To perform two-part arrangement, you will need seven groups, each with at least two players.

Procedure

- Lead students in a discussion of their understanding of *modes*—that a mode, like a scale, is a particular arrangement of tones, that pentatonic modes have five tones, that diatonic modes have seven, and that diatonic modes can be major- or minor-sounding.
- Show Phrygian, explaining that its distinctive sound comes from its particular arrangement of tones from E to E' on the keyboard.
- Show the "Spanish Phrygian mode" by including both G and G-sharp.
- Demonstrate fingering for G-sharp.
- Lead the students in the melodic progressions suggested on the Recorder Master, or other progressions involving G-sharp.
- Call attention to accidentals and meter changes in the piece. Explain that the solid bar lines after measures 3, 5, 10, as well as at the end of the piece, indicate a division of parts. Tell students to think of parts 2 and 5 as echoes of parts 1 and 4.
- Divide the class into seven groups and assign each of them a numbered part in the playalong.
- Let each group practice its short two-part phrase.
- Have students play the entire song.

Name ______________________________ Date ______________

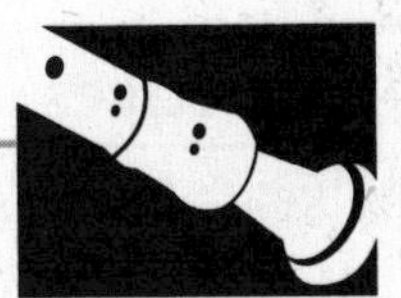

You Know More Than You Think You Know

Do you know instantly what this piece is when you look at it?

- Sing it first with pitch names. What is its home tone? Sing it with syllables:

  do re mi do do re mi do mi fa so— mi fa so—

- What intervals are in the melody? Play it as you think the syllables.
- Challenge yourself: start on F and play the same syllables. What is the key signature when F is *do?* Sing the pitch names and play it again. The fingering for both F and B-flat is hard.
- Start on E—E is *do,* F♯ is *re,* G♯ is *mi*. Sing the pitch names and finger silently.
- How about D for *do?* What is the key signature? Sing the names of the notes, then play.
- Just one more: C is *do*. What is the key signature? Sing, then play.

Write the phrases you played and the names of the keys in the staffs below.

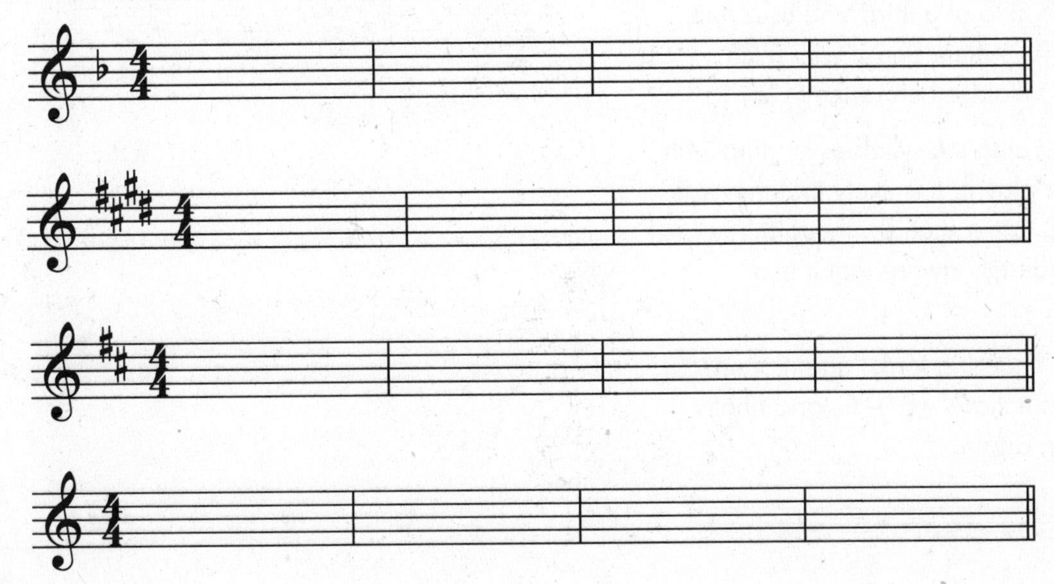

Pitches: C D E F F♯ G G♯ A B♭ B C' D'

Using Recorder Master R • 19

Objectives

- Students will review the 12 notes they know on the recorder by transposing a short well-known piece in G into the keys of F, E, D, and C.
- Students will notate the piece in the transposed keys.

Preparation

- Have students review fingering for F#, G#, and B♭.
- Review the three-part echo system: listen to the phrase to be echoed, sing the pitch names and finger silently, play the echo.

Procedure

- Remind students that they know how to play a large number of notes that appear in many scales, many pieces.
- Guide them in analyzing the two short phrases of "Frère Jacques." It moves in steps except for the skip of a third and uses five tones only. Have them sing it with pitch names, then syllables before they play it.
- Have students sing the syllables starting with F as *do,* then play it. It is likely that they will at first play B rather than B♭, though they will be immediately aware that it is a "wrong note."
- Demonstrate fingering for B♭ again, then have students echo A – B♭ – C, and finally play the song again.

- Follow the same procedure with the other keys, E, D and C, students singing the pitches before they play them.
- Before the exercise in E, review and demonstrate again fingering for F# and G# and have students echo such phrases as:

  E – F# – G# – E – G#

- "Frère Jacques" in E, D, and C:

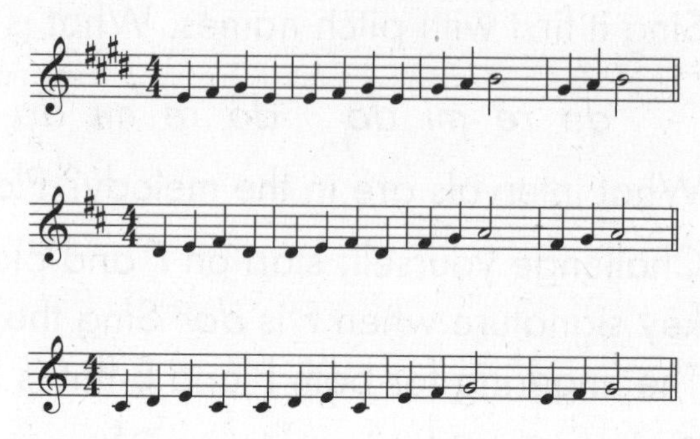

- Encourage students to solve the puzzle of which key they can use to play the whole song. Have them start the third phrase of "Frère Jacques" on *so* and try playing it by ear. F is the only key in which they can play both the third and fourth phrases:

Name ______________________ Date ______________

All in the Family

Today, let's become acquainted with the alto recorder.

- Begin by learning C', D', and E'.

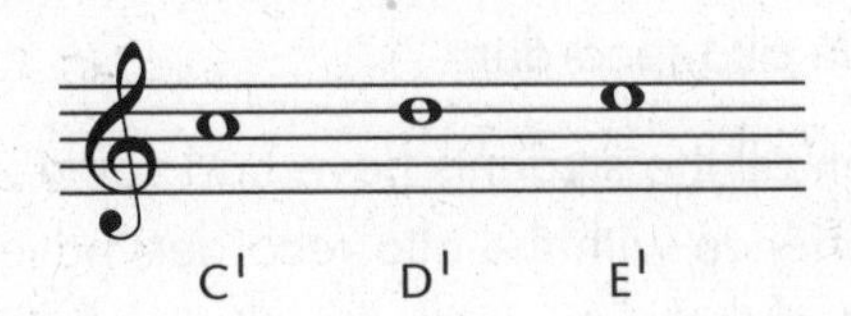

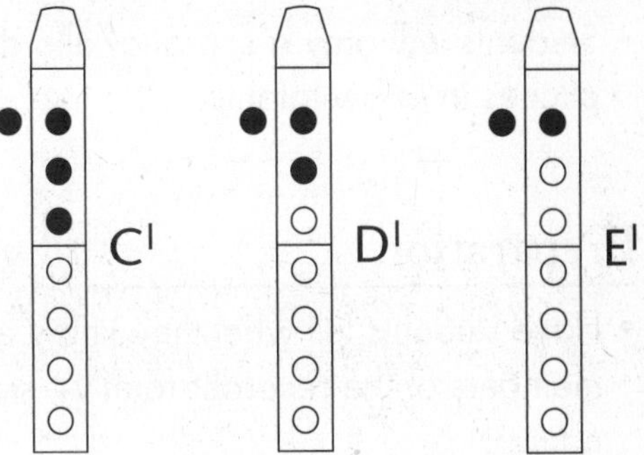

- The first note to learn with your right hand is A. Finger and sing the notes for D – C – A. When you can do this easily, play those notes on the alto recorder.

- Sing "Hullaballoo Balay" from your book.
- Does "Hullaballoo Balay" fit this pentatonic scale? Which other pitch is used?

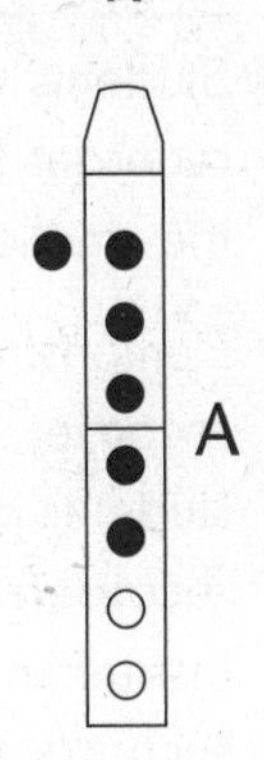

- When a piece has the syllables of a pentatonic scale and ends on *la* instead of *do,* we call it *La pentatonic* and it always has a minor sound.
- Soprano recorder players: Play these pentatonic pitches up and down: F G A C' D' C' A G F slowly; then repeat.
- Alto recorder players: Play three notes of the pentatonic scale with the soprano players:

- Play "Hullaballoo Balay" from your books.

Pitches: SR: C D F G A C' D' AR: A C' D' E'

Using Recorder Master R•20

Objectives

- Students will learn A C D E on the alto recorder.
- Students will play a soprano/alto duet using pitches in *la* pentatonic.

Preparation

- Have students tell what they know about members of the recorder family—sizes, names.
- Have students hold alto recorder in the same position as soprano recorder.

Procedure

- Students will discover that the larger recorder has a lower sound than the smaller.
- Demonstrate fingering for C D E on the alto recorder. (CAUTION: Take care that students do not transpose from the soprano recorder. They must think of this as a new instrument with its own fingering. Although such transposition might be easier at first, it quickly becomes a hindrance to their learning to play both soprano and alto instruments.)
- Guide students in playing "Mary Had a Little Lamb" by ear on alto recorder. Give students phrases on E D C to echo, then have them work in small groups to gain facility in echoing these three notes.
- Have students understand E D C as home base on the alto recorder. Demonstrate fingering for A and continue to echo phrases now including A with E D C.
- Have students sing "Hullaballoo Balay" from their books, then sing pitch names and finger silently the second line of the song on alto recorders. Notice that E is not needed.
- Have students sing the first and third lines with pitch names and play the second line on the alto recorder.
- When all the students have had some experience with the alto recorder, have some of them stay with the alto and others take out their soprano recorders.
- Discuss with students the *la* orientation (tonal center) of the syllables in the song. Note that the pentatonic scale has no *fa* and no *ti*, which in this case *fa* is B-flat and *ti* is E. Have students sing the first and last lines in syllables, and then identify its home tone *(D)* and whether it is a major or minor mode *(minor)*.
- Have students play the SR/AR exercise.

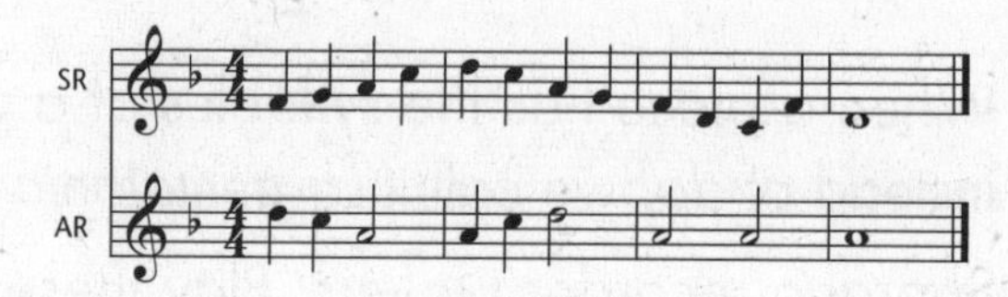

- Play "Hullaballoo Balay" as a soprano/alto recorder duet, soprano recorder on lines 1 and 3, alto recorder on line 2.

Name ______________________ Date ______________

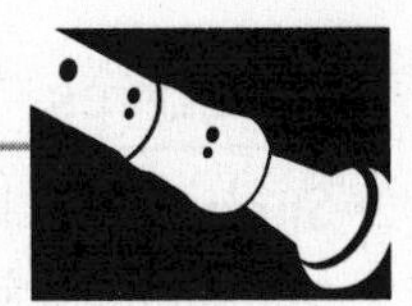

Another Set of Five

All the pentatonic scales you have studied so far have the following qualities:

1. They consist of the five tones, using syllables *do, re, mi, so,* and *la.*
2. They can have any key signature.
3. They have no half steps.
4. Their tonal center can be any one of the five syllables.

- Today we will learn a different scale from Japan, made up of these five tones:

- It's time now to learn C-sharp—an easy one to finger. Starting with the fingering for high D (left hand middle finger only, no covering of thumb hole), cover the first hole with pointer finger. Practice these progressions:

Dˡ C♯ˡ Dˡ   Dˡ C♯ˡ Cˡ C♯ˡ Dˡ

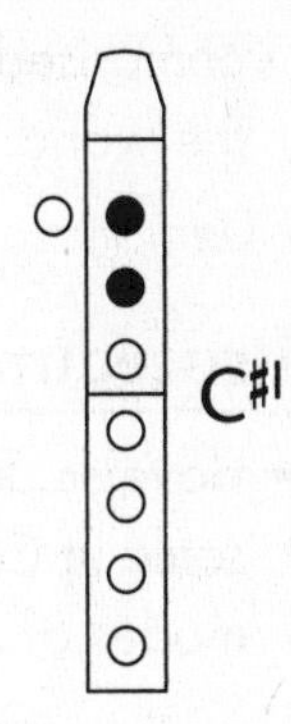

- Play the piece below on soprano recorder as an introduction and coda to "Sakura."

Virginia Nylander Ebinger

Pitches: D F♯ G B C♯ˡ Dˡ

Using Recorder Master R•21

Objectives

- Students will learn that, in addition to the pentatonic scales they have learned, there are many other different arrangements of five tones. They will learn one on which "Sakura" is built.
- Students will learn $C^{\#}$ on the soprano recorder.
- Students will play a piece as introduction and coda for "Sakura."

Preparation

- Discuss with students the pentatonic scale as they have studied it, its syllables, intervals, modes, especially *do, re,* and *la* modes.
- Explain that there are many other scales comprised of five tones scale throughout the world.

Procedure

- Have students sing syllables of pentatonic scale in C, D, and F, in *do, re,* and *la* modes of each.

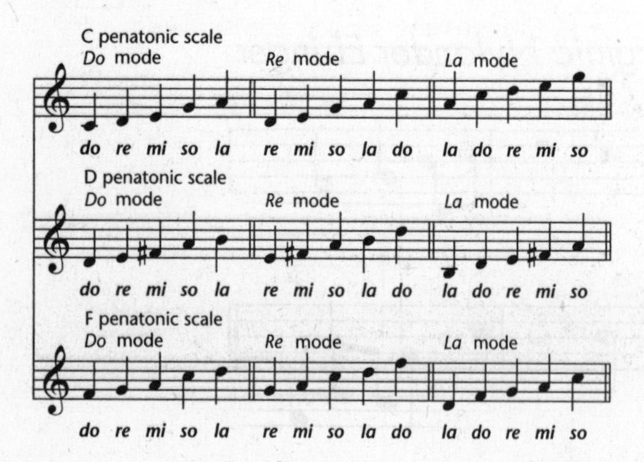

- Have students play *do* mode of C, D, and F pentatonic scales on soprano recorder.
- Demonstrate fingering for $C^{\#l}$ and play short phrases which include $C^{\#l}$ for students to echo, for example:

  D^{l} $C^{\#l}$ D^{l}

  D^{l} $C^{\#l}$ C^{l} $C^{\#l}$ D^{l}

  D^{l} $C^{\#l}$ B A G

- Have students play five-tone scale that is written on the Recorder Master (page 41). Alert students to the half steps between $F^{\#}$ and G, and $C^{\#}$ and D^{l}.
- Have students listen, then sing "Sakura," finally have them discuss the ways in which this song sounds different from most Western music.
- Have students play as an introduction and coda to "Sakura" the piece on the Recorder Master R•21.

Name ________________________________ Date ________________

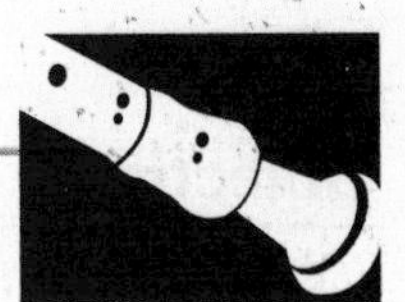

Ostinato, Rondo, and Two Recorders

Review the notes you have learned on the alto recorder: E' D' C' A.

Now for two more new alto recorder notes:

B

F#'

• Practice these three notes in various progressions:

D F# D B D F#   F# D F# B D and especially B D B F# F# B (this will be your ostinato).

Review the D pentatonic scale with the soprano recorder.

• Finger and sing, then play the D pentatonic scale up and down a few times, then in groups of four play question/answer games using these notes. Make your answers end on B. What syllable of the scale is B? When you end on B, do you get a major or a minor sound?

Now it's time for a rondo duet.

Pitches: AR: A B C D E F#'   SR: D E F# A B D'

Using Recorder Master R • 22

Objectives

- Students will learn to play B and high F♯ on the alto recorder and will use them in an ostinato accompanying a rondo.
- Students will learn a soprano recorder piece to use as the A section of a rondo and will improvise episodes.

Preparation

- Review known notes on alto recorder: E' D' C' A.
- Review reading in upper octave of the staff.
- Discuss and show range of alto and soprano recorders.

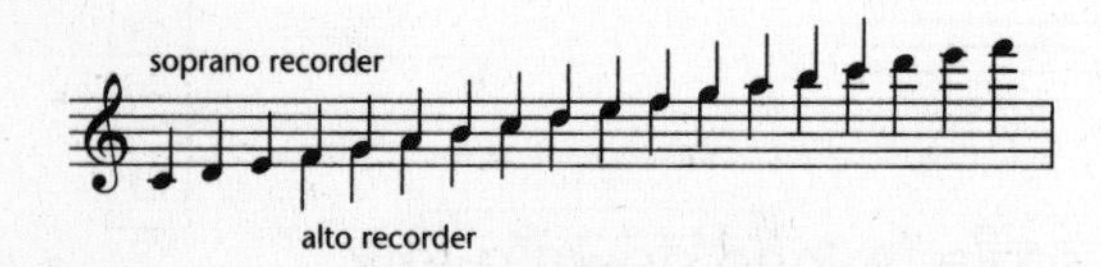

- Have a chart prepared showing D pentatonic scale, with stems indicating notes each instrument will be playing in this lesson.

Procedure

- Have students play chain echoes on alto E' D' C' A, as follows. Make two rows facing each other; number those in one row in odd numbers, the other in even numbers. Make a chain, playing across to each other in four beats each. At first odd numbers play a phrase for even numbers to echo. Then switch. The 4-beat echoes can be extended to 8-beats.
- Be sure every student has a turn at the alto recorder.
- Demonstrate alto fingering for B and high F♯.
- Have students practice echoing alto recorder phrases including B, D and F♯.
- Lead students in discussion about the major and minor sounds possible in the pentatonic scale: major—*do* is home tone; minor—*la* is home tone.
- Have students echo phrases on soprano recorder, emphasizing *la* pentatonic mode of D pentatonic scale.
- Give students musical questions to answer. Let your questions end on F♯ which will give an impetus for the students' improvisational answers.
- Have half the class learn alto recorder ostinato and play it throughout as the other half sings "Yüe líang wan wan." Change parts. Note that the ostinato continues three measures after the song is finished.
- Have students learn soprano recorder piece written on Recorder Master R•22. Combine alto and soprano recorder parts.
- Review the form of a rondo with students: it contains a recurring musical unit, called A, alternating with contrasting units (B, C, D, and so forth).
- Have students continue the alto recorder ostinato as soprano recorder players make a rondo, with A section the piece as written and the episodes improvised. Encourage students to end their improvisations on B, giving them a La-pentatonic feeling.

Name ______________________________ Date ______________

A Single Voice

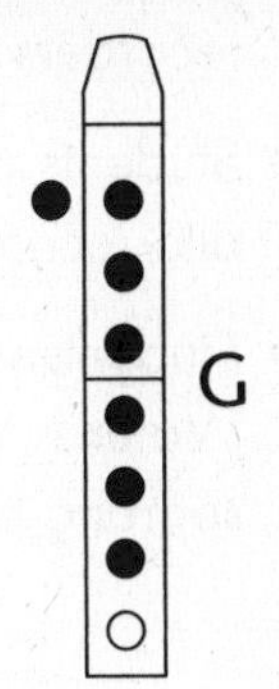

Unison—a single sound. We can achieve unison with two or more recorders playing on the same part at the same time. To obtain a pleasing sound, it is important to listen very carefully to each other while playing to play in tune, and to adjust to match each other's tuning. Try first to tune the soprano recorders, then alto recorders in the same way.

Learn this fingering for G on alto recorder. The pitch G can be played by both soprano and alto recorders.

Perform the playalong for "The Water Is Wide," without the song at first, then with the song.

Try this descant, also possible for either soprano or alto recorder.

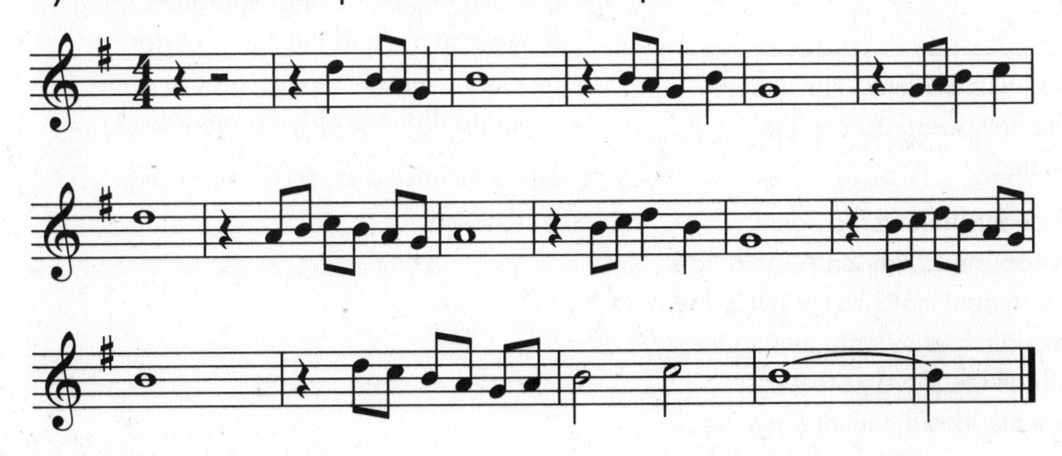

Pitches: G A B C' D'

Using Recorder Master R•23

Objectives

- Students will learn how to tune their recorders to a unison pitch.
- Students will learn fingering for G on alto recorder.
- Students will perform a playalong for "The Water Is Wide" on pitches common to both soprano and alto recorders.

Preparation

- Have students review fingering and echo on either instrument phrases containing G A B C' and D' and containing long notes.
- Call attention to breath control, especially on long notes which tend to drop in pitch unless players maintain breath support.
- Review chart on Recorder Master R•22 showing range for soprano and alto recorders.

Procedure

- Discuss unison with students. Have them talk about the first paragraph on the Recorder Master.
- Work with students to tune recorders, starting with sopranos. Play an A, holding it while the first student matches the pitch, then other students join one by one, aiming for a unison A with all the soprano recorders playing. Students should continue joining and holding the tone, but teacher should stop playing in order to help students who need it. If a student's pitch is flat, it may be helped by blowing a little harder. If it is sharp, try adjusting by pulling the top of the recorder out a little bit.
- When the sopranos are in tune, work with the altos in the same way.
- Finally, try to tune all the instruments to each other.
- Demonstrate fingering for G on alto recorder.
- Alert students that soprano and alto recorders can play some, but not all of the same notes. The alto recorder cannot play the pitches E D C, playable by the soprano recorder, nor can the soprano play the highest pitches the alto can play, but both of them can play all those in between—F to C''.
- Finger silently, holding notes to full value, the playalong for "The Water Is Wide." Both soprano and alto instruments are able to play this piece together.
- Play the playalong without the song, paying special attention to maintaining pitch on the long notes.
- Combine the playalong, soprano and/or alto recorders, and the song, performed by the class divided into two groups (those singing and those playing recorders).
- Guide interested students in playing the descant.

Name ______________________ Date ______________

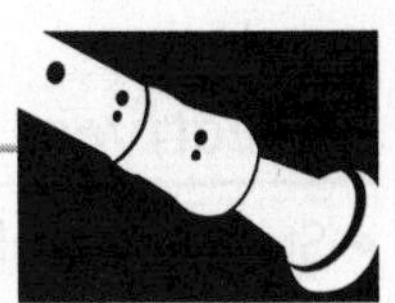

Then and Now

Here is that melody for "Belle Qui Tiens Ma Vie" with a playalong. First learn this new note on the alto—B-flat.

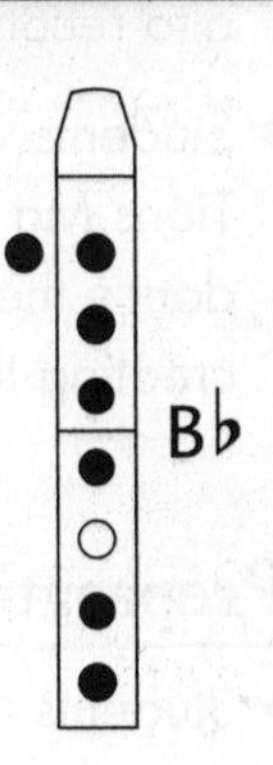

- Describe the mood of this piece. What is its form? Do you think it is major or minor? What is the pitch of the tonal center?
- Now it's your turn to compose your own pavane. Here are some helping rules:

  Instrument: soprano recorder.
  Form: A A B B, each part four measures.
  Inner form: Question/answer in each part.
  Key: G minor. (Use an F or F♯ if you want to; do not use E or E♭)
  Other: Let your question end on D, your answer on G.

- Work in groups of four to compose your pavane.

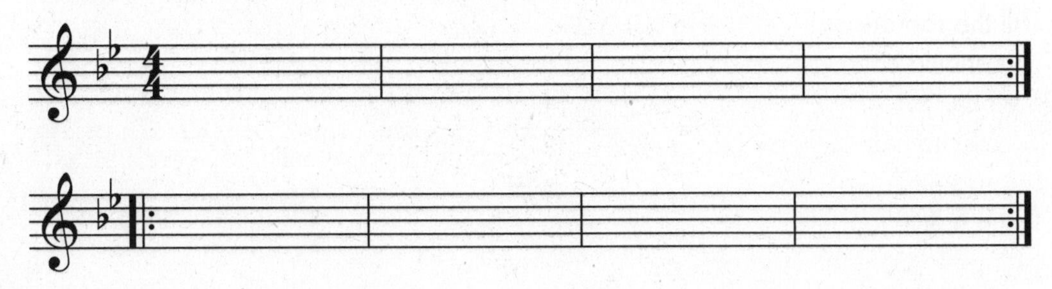

Pitches: SR: D E F F♯ G A B♭ C' D' AR: G A B♭ C' D'

Using Recorder Master R•24

Objectives

- Students will learn fingering for B-flat on alto recorder.
- Students will learn playalong for "Belle Qui Tiens Ma Vie," play it for other students to dance the pavane, and analyze it to aid in creating their own pavane.

Preparation

- Students will practice echos on soprano recorder including: G – F♯ – G; B♭ – D – C – B♭; B♭ – A – B♭; G – F♯ – G; and D – E – F – G.

Procedure

- Guide students to discuss what they know about music, dress, customs of the sixteenth and seventeenth centuries, referring to the illustrations and text in their books.
- Demonstrate fingering for B-flat on alto recorder. Have students echo phrases including: C' – B♭ – A; D' – C' – B♭ – A.
- Read and finger silently the soprano recorder part of "Belle Qui Tiens Ma Vie," then play it.
- Discuss the piece, its form, mood, mode, tonal center. (Students probably will not be familiar yet with the key signature for B♭ major, hence it would be enough, when they discover that G is the tonal center, just to tell them it is La. They will know that La indicates minor mode.)
- Have students practice alto recorder part, taking care that the B♭ is correctly fingered.
- Have students play both parts of the song. The second part may be played on the soprano recorder as well as on the alto.
- Divide the class so that half are dancers (who dance the pavane) and half play the "Belle Qui Tiens Ma Vie" arrangement for their dance. Change parts.
- Discuss with students the rules on Recorder Master R•24 for composing their pavane through question/answer activity.
- Have students form groups of four to compose and notate their piece.

Name ______________________________ Date ______________

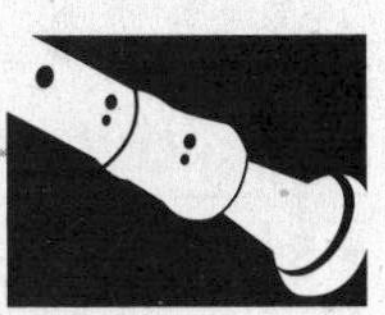

From Re to Dorian

• What do you see here? What is the difference between the first and second of these scales? If you look closely, you will see that both are pentatonic and have identical notes; their difference is simply in where they start and end, what their tonal centers are. The first is *do* pentatonic mode, the second is *re* pentatonic mode. Both have no flats and no sharps.

• In order to establish the sound of these modes, play first the *do* pentatonic mode up and down, then the *re* pentatonic mode up and down.

• The penta (five) tonic (tone) scale has steps 1 2 3 5 and 6, or *do re mi so* and *la*. These tones can be arranged so that any one is the home tone, the tonal center. When steps 4 and 7, *fa* and *ti*, are added, the result is a diatonic scale of seven tones.

• Now play these scales up and down. The first, from *do* to *do*, we call the major scale. The second, from *re* to *re*, we call the Dorian mode. Notice that they both use the same key signature of no sharps or flats. Play the *re* pentatonic mode, then the Dorian mode. Do they sound somewhat alike? Play "Round and Round" from your book and listen carefully to the "added" tones, F and B. Here is an ostinato playalong for the alto recorders while the sopranos play "Round and Round."

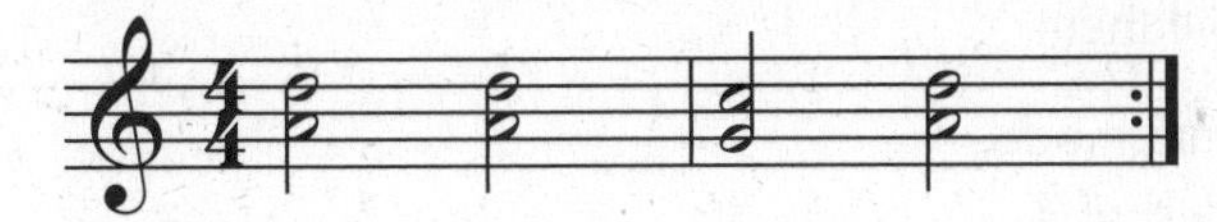

Pitches: SR: C D E F G A B C' D'   AR: G A C' D'

Using Recorder Master R•25

Objective

- Students will learn the relationship of *re* pentatonic mode to Dorian diatonic mode and will learn an ostinato for alto recorders to play with soprano recorders on "Round and Round."
- Students will perform the round in movement and music.

Preparation

- Lead students in discussion about the pentatonic scale. They should be quite familiar with *do* pentatonic.
- Prepare a chart with *do* and *re* pentatonic modes and C major and Dorian mode diatonics so that students can focus together rather than individually on their Recorder Master R•25 as they study these notes.

Procedure

- Have students study the two pentatonic modes on the chart, *do* and *re,* and explain what is alike and different about them.
- Have students play *do* pentatonic mode, then *re* pentatonic mode and describe difference in sound.
- Have students tell the difference between pentatonic and diatonic scales.
- Have students play the C major scale, then play the Dorian scale. Call their attention to the key signature—no sharps and no flats—which makes the notes in both scales exactly the same, but sounding very different because of different arrangement of whole steps and half steps and their tonal centers.
- Have students read and play "Round and Round" from their book, first in unison then in 3-part round.
- Read and play ostinato on alto recorder, then combine parts.
- Perform movement with music of the round. Have 3 or 4 alto recorder players in the center of a circle of the other students. Number off in this circle in 3s. Play and move as follows:
  - Part 1: 4 steps toward center (half note)
  - Part 2: 4 steps back in place.
  - Part 3: 4 steps turn around in place.
- Have students memorize the round, then play and move first in unison, then in a 3-part round.
- Page 286 in the student book has a Dorian song which may be of interest, and pages 210–211 have a Dorian song and a good explanation of the Dorian mode.

Name ______________________________ Date ____________________

Recorder Master R • 26

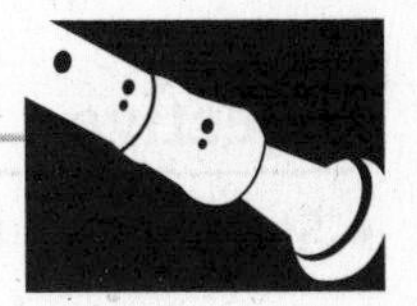

A Recorder Threesome

Play an arrangement in three parts of "Doney Gal."

Pitches: SR: D E F# G A B D' AR: G A B C' D' E'

Using Recorder Master R • 26

Objective

- Students will learn to play a trio arrangement of "Doney Gal."

Preparation

- Have students review fingering for alto recorder G through E' and soprano recorder G pentatonic plus F#.
- Lead students to discuss what they know about the life of a cowboy, the isolation and loneliness, and how it affected the music that came from the western cowboy culture.

Procedure

- Introduce students to the three part score of an arrangement of "Doney Gal."
- Guide students through the separate parts, as follows:
  1. Part I for soprano recorder: This is the song almost as it appears in the student book. Several times, usually at the beginning of sections, a pickup note, B below the staff, appears. This note cannot be played on either recorder, so in this arrangement it is simply replaced by a rest. Have students play the last section, marked with repeat signs, three times. Remind students to hold the half and dotted half notes their full time value.
  2. Part II for alto recorder: This is a descant full of long-held notes after the first section. It can be played on soprano recorder also.
  3. For Part III for alto recorder: This is a two-measure ostinato until the last two measures. Caution students to play this part in strict rhythm, not hurried.
- Divide students into groups of players and singers to perform the piece, with and without the recording. The recording will help to steady the tempo and keep the long notes lasting their full time value.
- Remind students to support their breath so their pitch will not drop.

Name ______________________ Date ____________

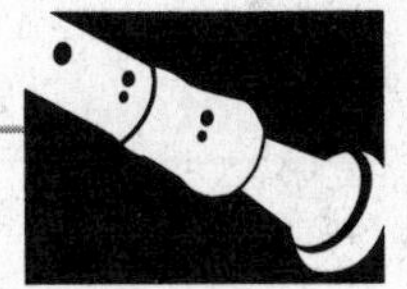

Major to Minor

Today let's look at *relative* and *parallel* minor.

Relative minor is *related* to a major key, having the same key signature, but lying a minor 3rd below the major.

Parallel minor has a different key signature but its melody moves in the same direction as the major key melody and has the same tonal center.

- Play "Hot Cross Buns" on your soprano recorder, then sing the syllables.

- Now look at the G major scale and sing all its syllables, beginning on *do*.

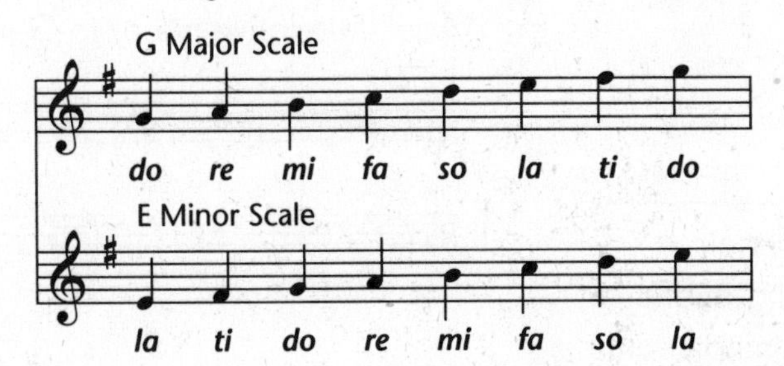

Now, go down a minor third from *do* (*do-ti-la;* G – F# – E). Sing a scale starting on *la,* and use the same key signature. This is the E minor scale. That is the *relative minor,* related to the major by the same key signature.

- Can you sing "Hot Cross Buns" in E minor, relative to G major? Look at the two scales above; draw a line from the three notes of the major scale used in the song to the three notes directly below in the minor scale; so your syllables are *do ti la.* Try singing the two parts together.

How do we get to a minor that is *parallel* to the major? It's that minor third again, but a minor third up rather than down (G – A – B♭). B♭ is *do*.

Pitches: E F# G A B♭ B C' D'

Using Recorder Master R•27

Objective

- Students will learn about parallel and relative minor modes and how to create them in reference to a given major scale and melody.

Preparation

- Have students practice and echo on soprano recorder the first five tones in G major (G A B C D), E minor (E F♯ G A B), and G minor (G A B♭ C D).

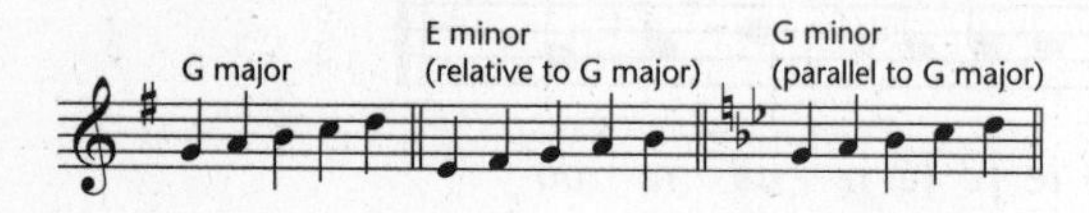

- Review with students minor thirds (three half steps).

Procedure

- Guide students through steps on their Recorder Master R•27 explaining and illustrating relative and parallel minors.
- Have students sing syllables in G major, E minor, and G minor for "Hot Cross Buns" and identify which of the minors they are singing.

- Point out to students the difference in the key signature: a minor third above G is B♭ the new *do*, making G the *la*, making the piece look, except for the key signature, exactly like G major, since the notes are on the same lines and spaces.
- Have students transfer this knowledge to "Winter Ade" and play both major and parallel minor versions as found in their book.
- Explain about relative and parallel major and how to find them.
- Have volunteers sing in syllables "Winter Ade" in relative major to G minor.

Name ____________________ Date ____________

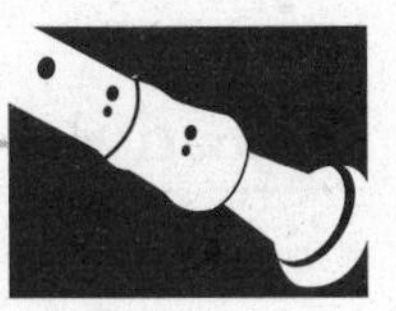

Steady and Strong

The basic element in the structure of a piece of music is the beat.

- Sing "The Lumber Camp Song" and pat the percussion part on the second staff: L R L R.

- Play the playalong on your soprano recorder.

- Is this accompaniment a strict ostinato? A short always repeating pattern? How does it help to keep the song moving and to keep everyone together?

Pitches: D G A C' D'

Using Recorder Master R•28

Objective

- Students will learn a playalong to "The Lumber Camp Song" that will strengthen their awareness that beat is the essential element that holds music together.

Preparation

- Have students echo rhythm patterns in $\frac{6}{8}$ meter, including dotted quarters, quarter-eighth, eighth-eighth-eighth.

Procedure

- Have students discuss how beat holds music together, the role of the conductor, ways of emphasizing beat.
- Have students sing "The Lumber Camp Song" while patting a steady beat on their legs. Ask them to identify the note value of the beat *(dotted quarter note)*.
- Have students pat percussion part while singing song.
- Have students choose a wooden percussion instrument and transfer this pattern to it. Have half the class stamp/clap the beat and half play the percussion part while all sing the song.
- Discuss ostinato and "modified" ostinato, after examining the percussion part in the playalong.
- Have students play the playalong on soprano recorder. Inform students that the first four measures are introduction, and all of it concentrates on beat.
- Divide the class so that some play the recorder, others play the percussion part, and others sing.
- Learn Orff Orchestration O•11 and put all the parts together.

Name ______________________________ Date ______________

Your Turn Now

Today's lesson is another soprano/alto duet in a playalong that includes many things—solos, a section of harmonic background, both instruments together with everybody playing *(tutti)*, and improvisations.

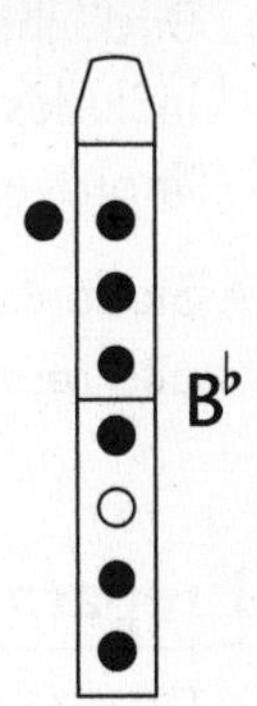

- Another note to learn on the alto recorder: B♭.
- Play this playalong for "Yellow Bird," following the teacher's directions.

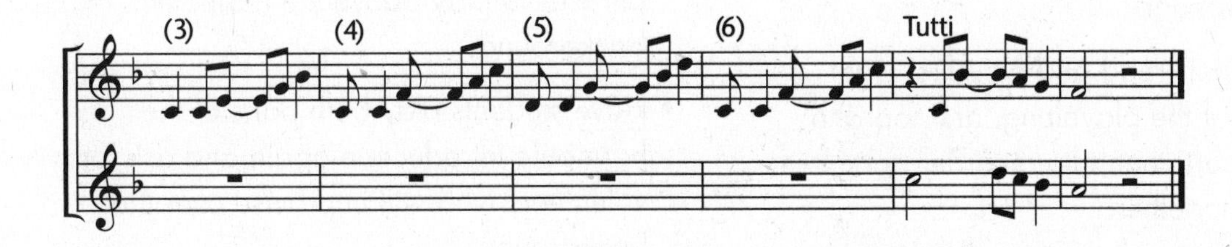

Pitches: SR: C D E F G A B♭ C' D' AR: G A B♭ B C' D'

Using Recorder Master R • 29

Objectives

- Students will learn a playalong to "Yellow Bird" that is a soprano/alto duet which includes solos, playing together, and improvisation over a given bass line.
- Students will learn how to play B on the alto recorder.

Preparation

- Discuss syncopation and have students create syncopated patterns for the class to echo over steady beat.
- Have students review alto fingering for C' – B – C' and A – B♭ – A – B♭ – C'

Procedure

- Have students sing "Yellow Bird," with or without the recording, patting the beat quietly while singing, paying attention to the way the syncopated patterns fit in and around the beat.
- Have students read and play first eight measures of the playalong, first soprano recorder part, then alto recorder part, then both together.
- Have students clap rhythm of all six solo parts, noting the slight difference between 1, 2, and 3 and 4, 5, and 6.
- Choose volunteers for each of the six solos. Give them a few minutes to practice their solos, and have the alto recorder players practice their part.
- The last two measures may be difficult to play together in the proper rhythm. This small section can be taken out and worked separately.
- Have students put the parts together in the playalong.
- Divide the class into two sections, one group to play the lower part of the first eight measures, the other group improvising all together. Have them start on the given note—A—then move mostly by steps up and down and around the next notes as they begin to improvise, only moving more independently when they feel secure. Change parts so that all have a chance to improvise.
- Divide the improvising group into pairs and have them work out question/answer phrases to play above the harmonic background.
- Have students play both parts of the harmonic introduction again and ask for volunteers who will improvise over that background.

Name ______________________________ Date ________________

Notes With Two Names

In music we have certain notes that sound alike but are written differently, called *enharmonics.*

A half step is the distance between two notes with no other note between them; a whole step is the distance between two notes with one note in between them. *A whole step is composed of two half steps.*

Half steps on a keyboard are easy to see: They fall between E and F and between B and C on the white notes, and every black note is a half step from at least one white note—C to C♯, D to D♯, F to F♯, G to G♯, A to A♯.

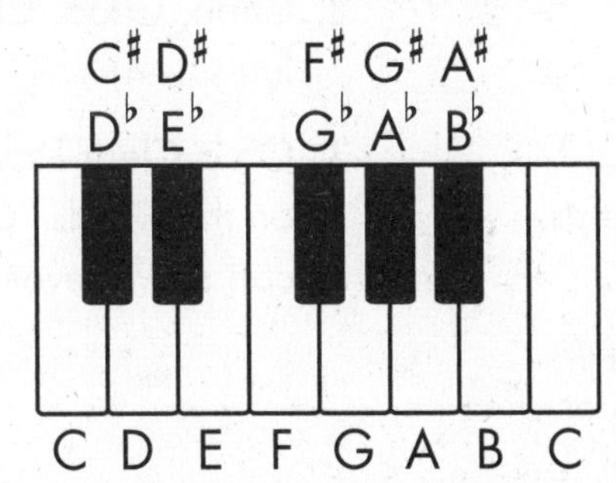

What if you start near the top of the scale and name the black and white half steps going down? Then you have B to B♭, A to A♭, G to G♭, E to E♭ and D to D♭. You don't have ten different black notes; instead you have two names for each of the five black notes: C♯ = D♭, D♯ = E♭, F♯ = G♭, G♯ = A♭, A♯ = B♭. These are *enharmonics.*

Let's look at some examples from your book. Find the notes with accidentals and name their enharmonic equivalent.

- It Don't Mean a Thing (page 164, line 1)
- Choo, Choo, Ch' Boogie (page 180, lines 1–4)
- On a Clear Day (page 207, lines 2–3)

With a partner discover how many half steps you can play and name enharmonically. Look for enharmonic notes in other songs and learn to "translate" them quickly into their other names.

Pitches: C D E F F♯ G G♯ A B♭ C' C♯' D

Using Recorder Master R•30

Objective

- Students will learn to identify and name enharmonic notes found in various songs.

Preparation

- Students will need to see a keyboard, either an actual keyboard or a pictured keyboard that shows at least one octave C to C for clearest identification of half steps and enharmonic tones.
- Review half steps and whole steps.

Procedure

- Students will identify and name half steps by sight on a keyboard.
- Students will identify and play the half steps they know on soprano recorder: F to F♯, G to G♯, B to B♭, C' to C♯'.
- Students will identify and play the half step they know on alto recorder: B to B♭.
- Show how each black note on the keyboard has two names, a sharp and a flat.
- Explain that the different range of soprano and alto recorders makes some notes easier to play on one than on the other.
- Have students identify and name both names of the enharmonic notes on the songs referenced from the student book:

1. It Don't Mean a Thing (page 164, line 1)

2. Choo, Choo, Ch' Boogie (page 180, lines 1–4)

3. On a Clear Day (page 207, lines 2-3, on the words "On that clear day, You can see forever, And ever more!")

Name ____________________ Date ____________

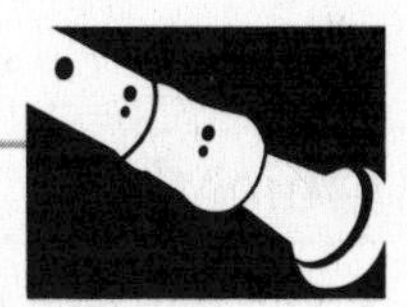

A Song From Long Ago

Look closely at "Sweet and Low," and find the short curved lines below the notes. These are *slurs* and they have at least two purposes. First, a slur can indicate that a word or syllable is to be sung on all the notes under that slur. A slur also can indicate a special articulation (tonguing) for recorder players. Instead of approaching each note with *doo* and closing it with a *t* (placing the tip of your tongue against the roof of your mouth), a slur tells you to create the sounds under it with one *doo—oo—t,* with no closure until the end of the slur. Try these examples:

- Can you hear in example 2 the difference your slurred notes and those with individual tonguing? Practice until you can hear the slurred notes.
- Notice the second note in example 3. What is the enharmonic equivalent of A-flat?
- Now for a playalong that provides a steady beat around which the tune can weave. Watch out for the Fs and the F-sharps. Since the key signature is C—no flats, no sharps—anytime an F sharp is called for, there must be an *accidental* placed before the F.

Pitches: D E F F♯ G G♯ A B C' D'

Using Recorder Master R • 31

Objectives

- Students will learn to articulate slurs on the recorder.
- Students will learn a playalong to "Sweet and Low."

Preparation

- Discuss slur markings and explain that they have multiple functions. The two most important uses for us are to indicate when more than one note is to occur on a syllable and also to indicate a different articulation for recorder players.

Procedure

- Demonstrate playing two notes with one approach: *doo—oo—t*. Demonstrate the difference in two notes slurred and two notes with separate tonguing.
- Have students practice playing slurs on adjacent notes. Caution students to keep tone supported with the breath so that the pitch doesn't drop, and also be careful not to jolt or punch the second tone.
- Have students read and play on soprano recorders the playalong, then divide the class into groups of singers, players of the song, and players of the playalong. Change parts so that all have each experience.

Name ______________________________ Date ______________________

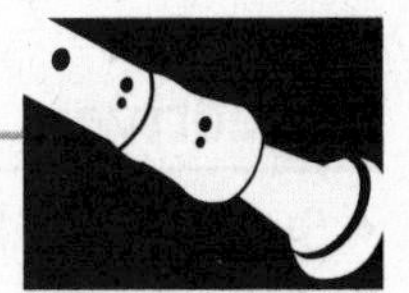

More Notes and Another Mode

Let's begin by learning two new notes on the alto recorder: F^I and G^I. They are among the easiest to play, and you will be happy to have them at your service.

The mode for today is Mixolydian, which is similar to the Dorian mode. Both modes have major and minor elements. Both modes have the same key signature, in this case, no flats and no sharps. Their half steps occur at different places (between E and F, B and C) within their tonal arrangement, and their tonal centers are different.

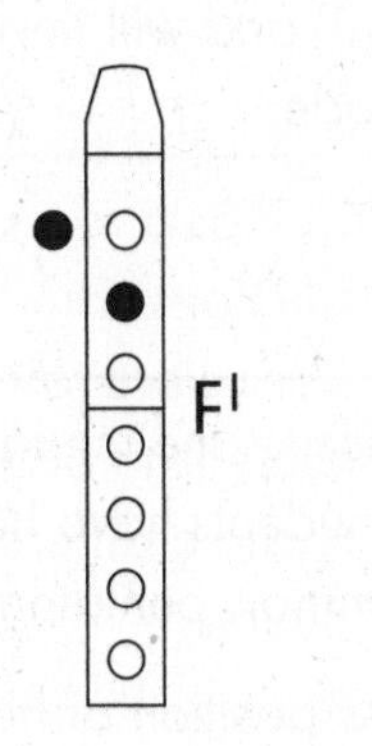

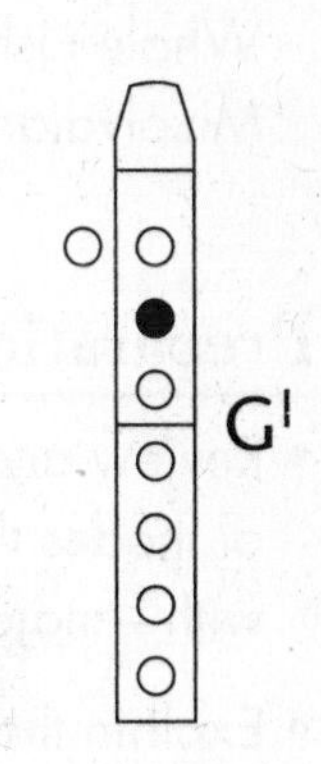

- Try Dorian mode on soprano and then Mixolydian on alto:

- Play the song in five groups, following your teacher's directions.
- Improvise: in your group of five, with either an alto or soprano recorder, follow the form of "The Greenland Whale Fishery," but create your own phrases.

  Player 1: improvise an 8-beat phrase that must include an F.

  Players 2, 3, 4: each improvise an 8-beat phrase that must include a B.

  Player 5: improvise an 8-beat phrase that must include an F. End the phrase on G.

Pitches: SR: D E F G A B C^I D^I AR: G A B C^I D^I E^I F^I G^I

Using Recorder Master R • 32

Objectives

- Students will learn high F and high G on the alto recorder.
- Students will study the structure of the Mixolydian modes.
- Students will learn a song, "The Greenland Whale Fishery," and will improvise in the Mixolydian mode.

Preparation

- Review and discuss the meaning and types of modes the students have had experience with—major, minor, pentatonic, Dorian.
- Explain that the position of half and whole steps is the determining factor of a mode.

Procedure

- Demonstrate fingering for $F^{\prime}$ and $G^{\prime}$ on alto recorder.
- Give students phrases to echo on the alto recorder: $G^{\prime}$ – $F^{\prime}$ – $G^{\prime}$; $G^{\prime}$ – F – E – $F^{\prime}$ – $G^{\prime}$; and other phrases including these two new notes.
- Review and discuss with students the structure of the Dorian mode, its minor sound because of the minor 3rd created by F and its major sound because of the major 6th created by B. Point out that these intervals are named in relation to D, the tonal center.
- Have students play the Dorian mode on soprano recorder.
- Introduce and discuss the structure of the Mixolydian mode (home tone G) also with major and minor elements created by F (a minor 7th above G) and B (a major 3rd above G).
- Have students play the Mixolydian mode on alto recorder.
- Have students play "The Greenland Whale Fishery" on soprano recorder. They should understand that playing the entire mode is easier on the alto recorder, but the notes of this song lie more in the range of the soprano recorder.
- Have students analyze the Mixolydian song, looking for the number of phrases, which sound similar to major, which sound similar to minor, and the notes in each phrase that give that effect.
- Divide class into five groups, preferably with five in each group. Assign one phrase (8 measures) to each group to play on soprano recorder, each group playing in succession without pause. Remind students that each phrase begins with a pickup beat.
- Have groups work alone on plan for improvised song according to the Recorder Master, then perform improvisation for the entire class.

Name ______________________ Date ____________

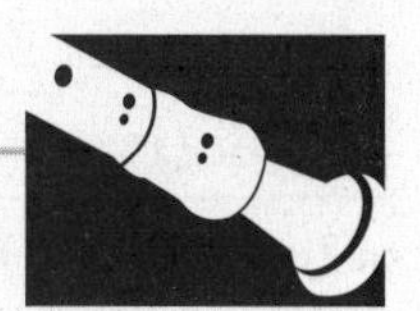

Working Together

Today's lesson puts together two songs from Greece, "Tsakonikos" and "Yerakina," in at least four different activities: dance, Orff instruments, soprano recorders, and alto recorders.

- *Dance.* Your teacher will review the movement for these two songs.
- *Orff instrument players.* Listen to the recording for "Tsakonikos" and perform 2 + 3, then 3 + 2 pat/clap patterns as you listen. This will prepare you for the instrumental parts. Then listen to the recording of "Yerakina" and practice 3 + 2 + 2 patterns as you listen.
- *Soprano recorder players.* Play "Yerakina" in the key of F.

- *Alto recorder players.* Play "Tsakonikos."

Pitches: SR: F G A B♭ C' D' AR: G A B C' D' E'

Using Recorder Master R•33

Objectives

- Students will learn to play two Greek dances, to combine them with Orff instruments, and to play for dancing.

Preparation

- Have students practice body percussion patterns: 3 + 2 + 2; 3 + 2; and 2 + 3 in pat/clap, snap/clap, or other two-level pattern.

Procedure

- Have entire class participate in each segment of this lesson—dances, alto recorder, soprano recorder, Orff Orchestration.
- Guide students through steps of their Recorder Master R•33. This lesson probably will require more than one class session to complete.
- Dances. Review "Tsakonikos" (teacher book, p. 215) and "Yerakina" (student and teacher books, p. 217). Form two groups, each spending a few minutes reviewing each dance. Dance both dances to the recordings.
- Orff Orchestrations for "Tsakonikos." After practicing body percussion parts, use the arrangement on pages 214, 215 in textbook.

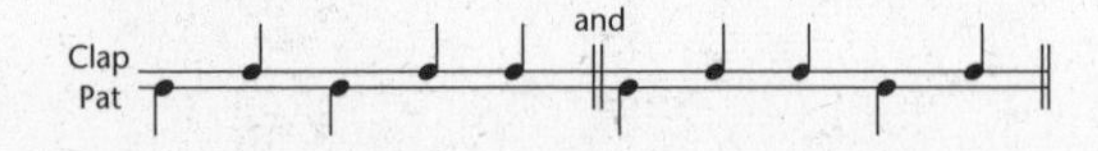

- Orff Orchestration for "Yerakina," O•14. Teach pat/clap pattern as the basic rhythm for the entire piece. Then teach parts in the following order:
  AX/BX
  HD
  Castanets
  SG/AG
  Tambourine (occurs only on "droom")
  Timpani

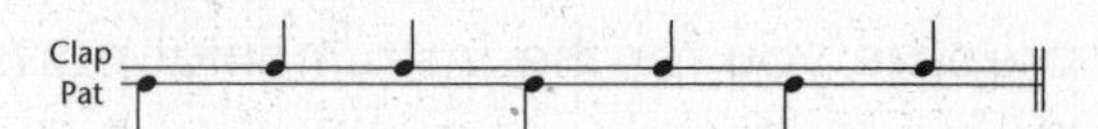

- Soprano recorder. Have students read and play "Yerakina." It will be helpful if they are accompanied by body percussion part. Combine with Orff Orchestration O•14.
- Alto recorder. Have students read and play "Tsakonikos." Have body percussion players accompany. Combine with Orff instrument arrangement in textbook.
- Combine dancers, recorder players, and Orff instrument players.

Name ______________________ Date ____________

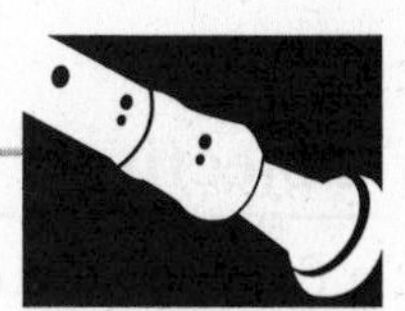

Keep On Rockin'

You have discovered that to analyze pieces, and to take small sections out and learn them separately, helps to master the music you are working on. Try that with "Rock Around the Clock."

- With a partner analyze the song by discussing these questions: (1) What is the meter? (2) What is the key? (3) Do all the notes match the key signature or are there some altered notes? (4) Are there repeated patterns? (5) Are there rhythmic difficulties that need separate practice?
- Here is a possible performance routine for four groups of soprano recorder players:

Introduction, Interlude:

Song:

Improvisation: Volunteers improvise over Interlude background.

- The pickup notes between phrases are omitted here. Add them by ear if you want to.

Pitches: D (E) F F♯ G A C'

Using Recorder Master R•34

Objective

- Students will analyze the parts of a piece as an efficient means to learning to play it.

Preparation

- Have students practice echoes to the following patterns.

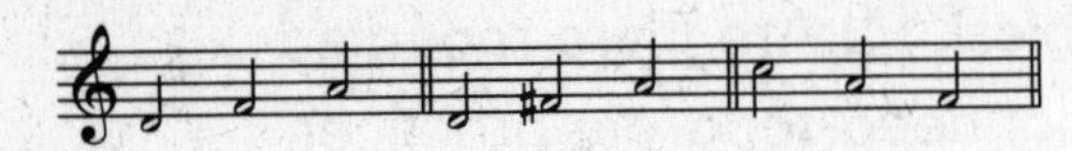

Procedure

- Guide students in discussing questions on Recorder Master concerning analysis of "Rock Around the Clock."
- Divide the class into four sections. Have each group practice the appropriate part, then combine to perform the piece as suggested.
- Encourage improvisation over D major triad.

Name ______________________ Date ______________

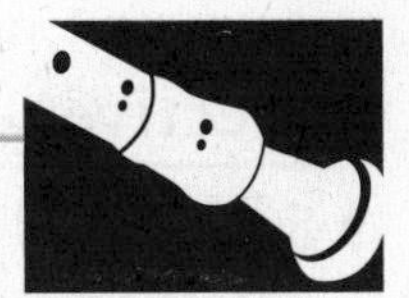

A Patriotic Song

There are many occasions for which patriotic songs are appropriate—to sing and to play on a variety of instruments. Here is perhaps the most well-known of all American patriotic songs. Play it as a soprano recorder solo or as a soprano and alto duet.

Pitches: SR: E F G A B♭ C' D'   AR: A B♭ C' D' E' F'

Using Recorder Master R • 35

Objective

- Students will learn to play a well-known patriotic song, "America," both as a solo and in an alto and soprano recorder duet arrangement.

Preparation

- Have students sing "America."
- Have students echo phrases that include F and B♭:

Procedure

- Play soprano and alto parts separately, then as a duet.

Name ____________________ Date ____________

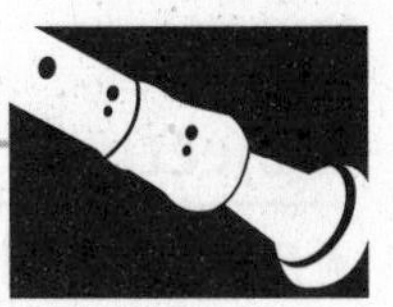

A Christmas Carol

"Les anges dans nos campagnes" ("Angels We Have Heard on High") is a well-known French Christmas carol.

Pitches: SR: C D E F G A B♭ C' D'   AR: C' D' E' F'

Using Recorder Master R • 36

Objective

- Students will learn to play "Les Anges dans nos Campagnes" ("Angels We Have Heard on High") as a soprano recorder solo and as a soprano/soprano/alto recorder trio.

Preparation

- Have students sing song.

Procedure

- Have students analyze piece: meter, key, possible rhythmic difficulties.
- Have students play soprano recorder 1 part.
- Have students play soprano recorder 1 and 2 together, then all three parts.

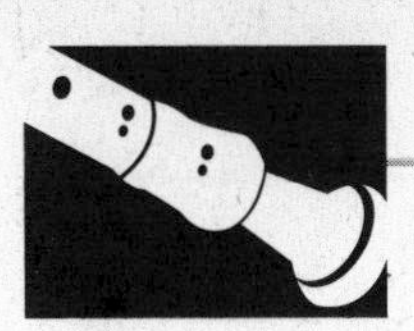

Index of Songs

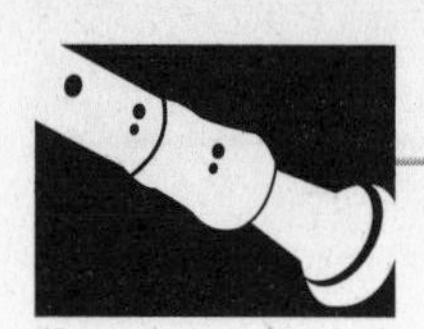

Soprano Recorder Fingering Chart

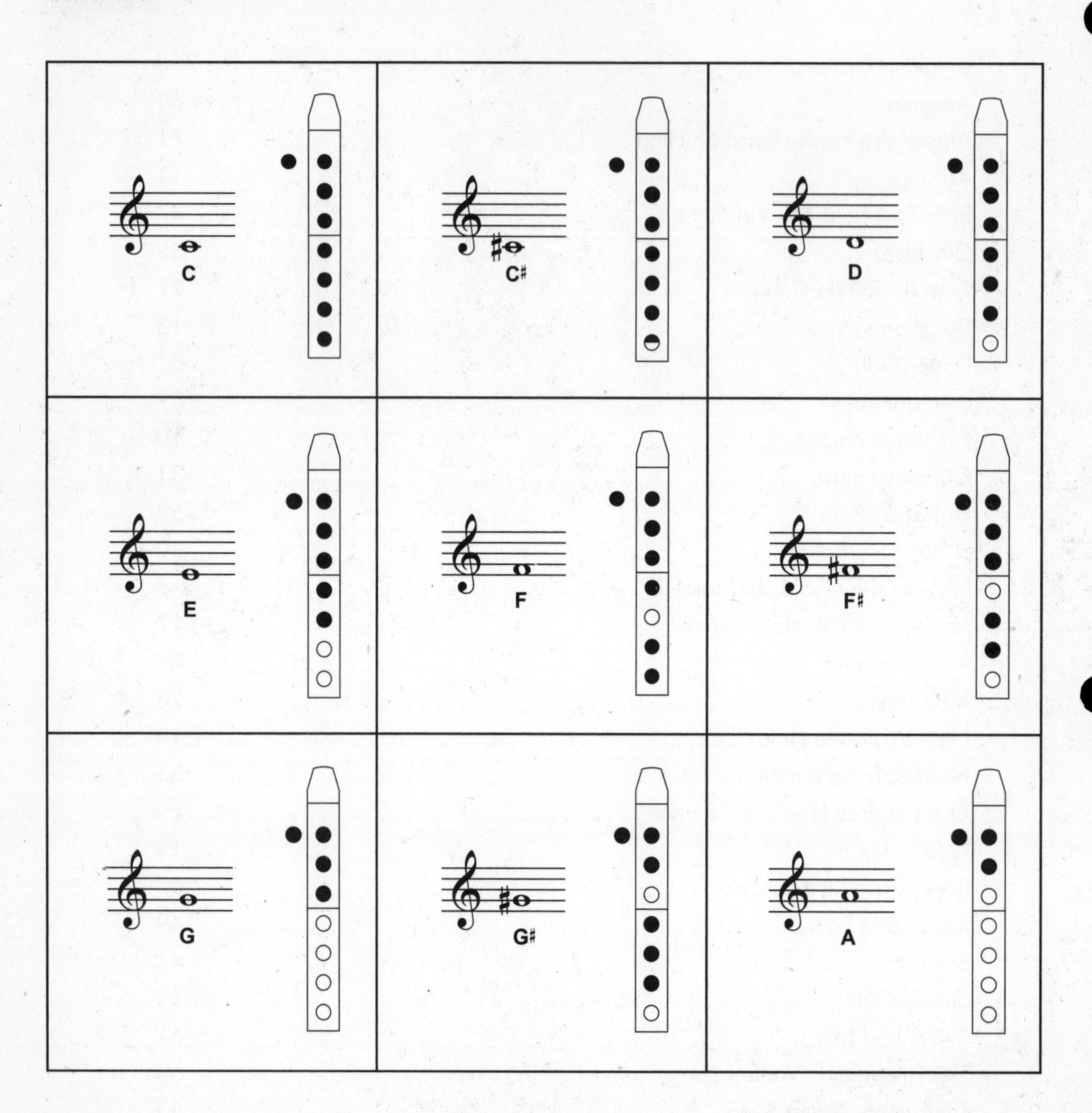

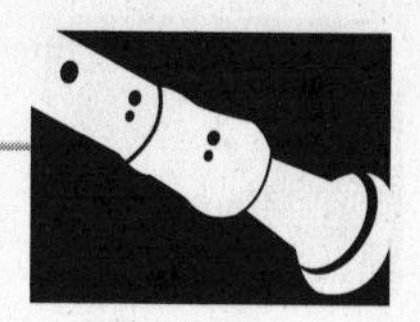

Soprano Recorder Fingering Chart (continued)

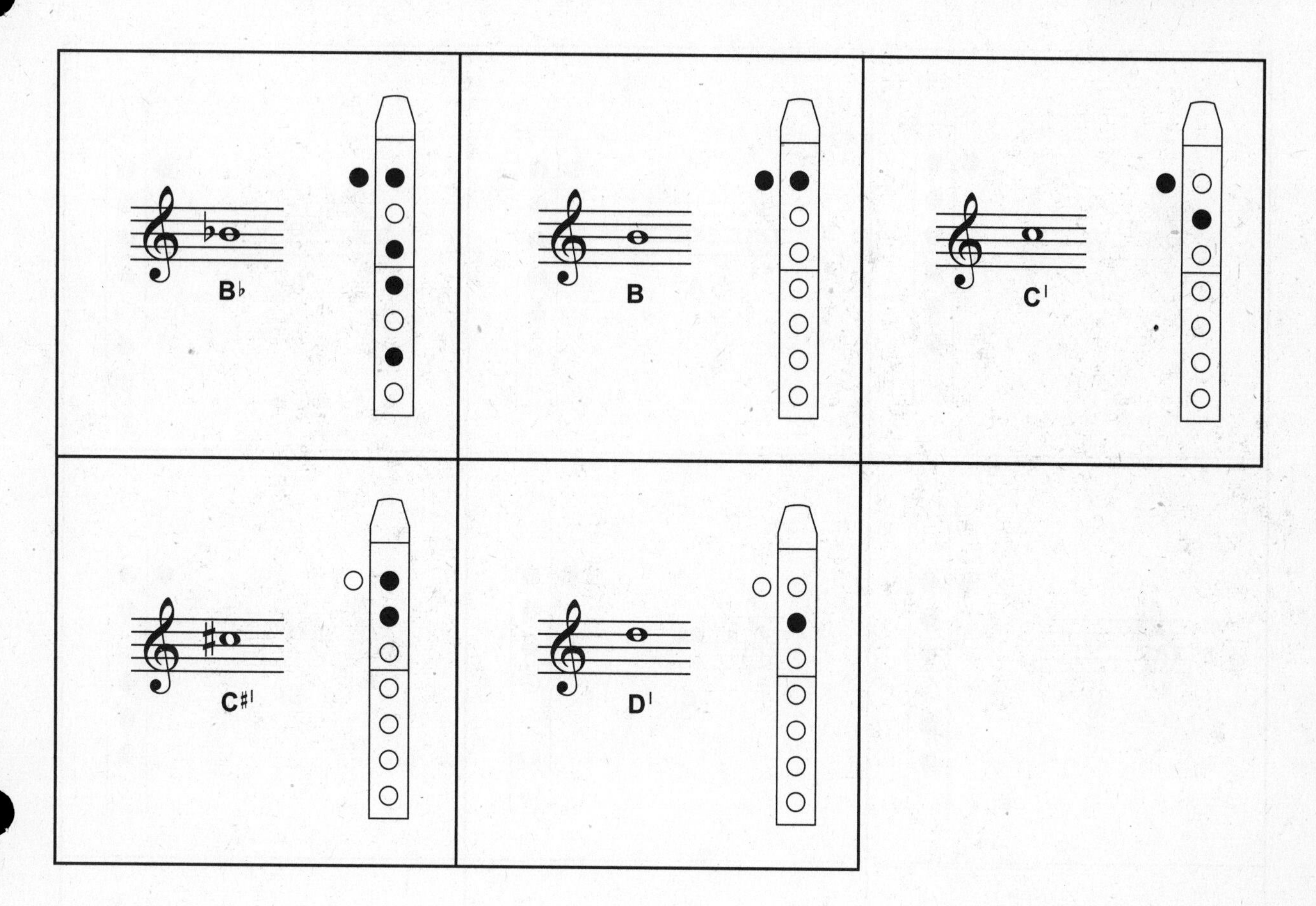

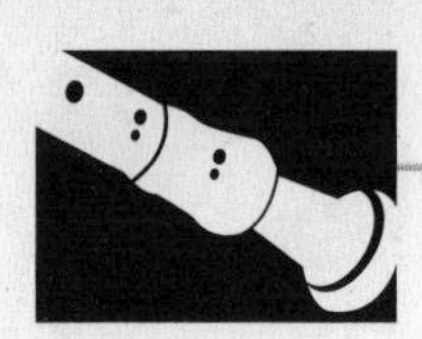

Alto Recorder Fingering Chart

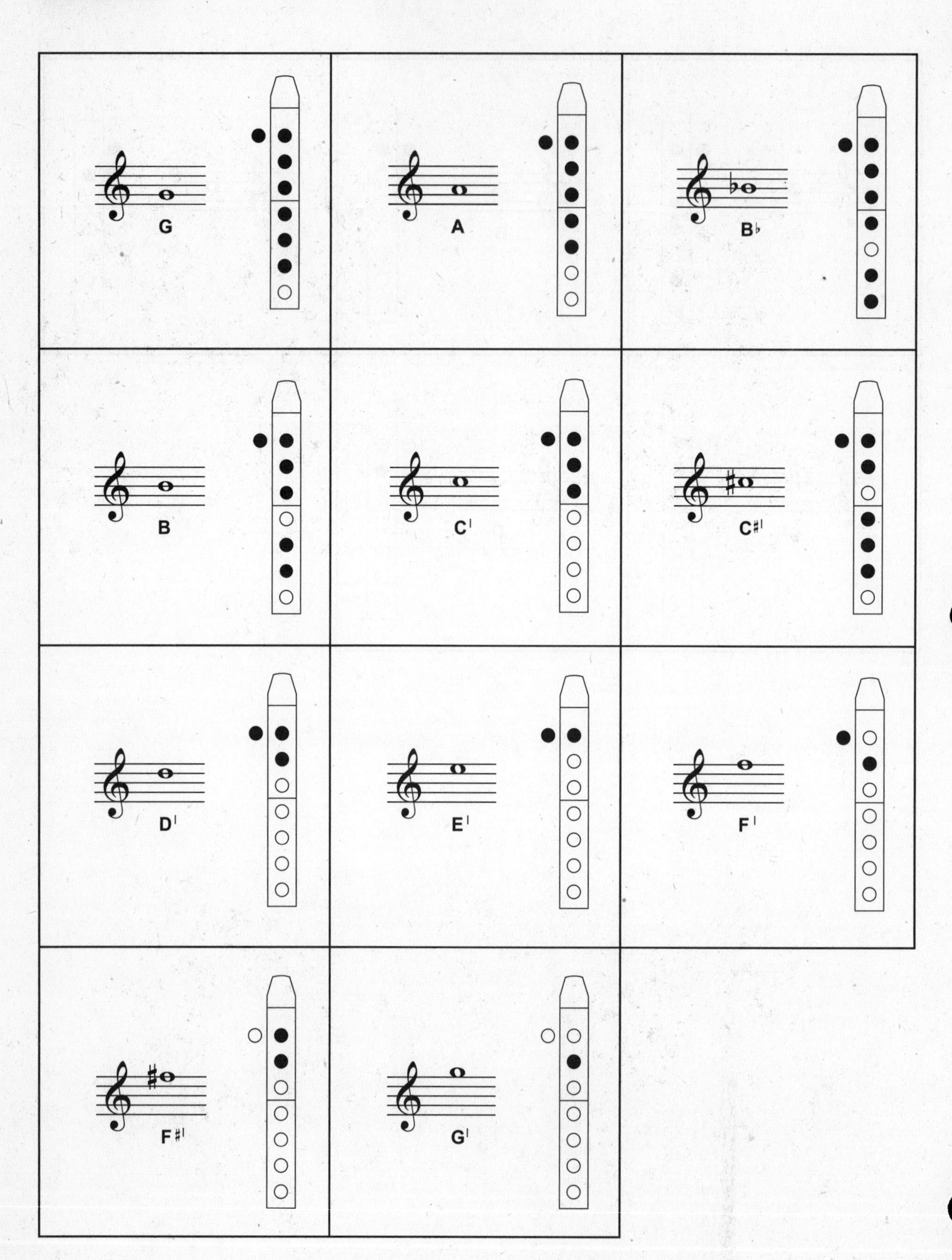